# SWALLOW A
# OF D

CW01646987

What you may not know
– is that once there was
Prince of Darkness rebel
content with his bit of time. He wanted more. He wanted all. He looked at the evil he managed to work in the few hours allotted to him and reasoned that if all time were his, there would be no end to his achievements.

Night by night, darkness advanced. In no time at all the whole northern half of the world was in his grasp; and whenever a day came to its end creatures drew together and prayed that it might not be their last.

For Tom

# SWALLOW AND THE PRINCE OF DARKNESS

John Livesey

A TARGET BOOK
*published by*
the Paperback Division of
W.H. Allen & Co. PLC

A Target Book
Published in 1986
by the Paperback Division of
W.H. Allen & Co. PLC
44 Hill Street, London W1X 8LB

Copyright © John Livesey, 1986

Printed and bound in Great Britain by
Cox & Wyman Ltd, Reading

ISBN 0 426 20215 5

This book is sold subject to the condition that it shall not, by way of trade or otherwise, be lent, re-sold, hired out or otherwise circulated without the publisher's prior consent in any other form of binding or cover other than that in which it is published and without a similar condition including this condition being imposed upon the subsequent purchaser.

# 1

# Sergeant Watt's Helmet

There was no doubt about it, the Swallow definitely had designs on the helmet. No sooner had Uncle Chris removed his policeman's helmet and hung it up on the peg on the wall, than the little bird had appeared from nowhere and perched on the top of the trellis a couple of yards away, eyeing it intently. While Tom and Jenny stood by and watched, he did no more than this; but the moment they began to move off to join their uncle on the lawn, he hopped off his perch and into the helmet. He now lay there, hidden save for his beak, half his head, and one eye which peaked at them over the rim.

'Uncle Chris! Uncle Chris!' they cried as they raced down the lawn. 'Uncle Chris, the Swallow's gone into your helmet.'

'Hmm – early this evening,' was their uncle's only reply as he lowered his aching body into the deckchair.

'You mean he's done it before?' asked Jenny.

'One of them has. Either him or another.'

'Is that why you leave it there – so they can sleep in it?' Tom demanded.

'Well, they seem to expect it,' his uncle replied, reaching for his mug of tea, and hoping to put them off by his evident lack of interest.

But the children's curiosity was aroused. 'Why?' they demanded in unison. 'Tell! Tell!'

It had been a long hot day and police sergeant Christopher Watt had spent most of it on his feet in or around Trafalgar Square, trying to decide which he disliked more – the Pigeons or the tourists. And now he had come home feeling as though his feet had grown two sizes too big for his boots, and his shirt had been cling-wrapped to his back. He didn't want to explain about the Swallows and his helmet. If he *could* explain. Heaven knew he'd tried to explain it to himself often enough – since that day, years ago, when he had casually hung his helmet on the wall in order to do something – he'd long forgotten what – and had come back to find it occupied by a bright, winking Swallow, who made no attempt to vacate the premises on the owner's return. And he, the owner, had felt rather flattered that the little bird should so honour him. So there the helmet had stayed. And there it had hung every summer evening since – unexplained and, for him, inexplicable. Yet the ritual cry of 'Tell! Tell!' demanded that an explanation be found. He cursed himself for ever starting this story-telling game with the children. But start it he had, and two pairs of expectant eyes told him now was not the time to stop.

'It's a long story,' he said, 'and Auntie Sarah will be calling you in soon.'

'Tell! Tell!' they insisted.

He was trapped and he knew it. His only hope – a last minute rescue by Sarah calling them in to tea – was forlorn; timing had never been Sarah's strong point. Had the soldiers in many an Indian-beset fort in a Western depended on Sarah's riding to their rescue, then they would have died disappointed, and an Apache Administration would long since have been installed in the White (renamed 'Red') House. With the pessimism born of long experience he resigned himself to his fate, and was settling begrudgingly back to attempt his explanation, when to his confusion the French windows were flung open and out charged Sarah's Seventh Cavalry.

'Tea's ready. Come and wash your hands.'

Fort Watt was relieved! The two besieging Red Indians were despatched fleeing to the bathroom, and the beleaguered sergeant breathed freely again. It had been a close call.

He laid his head back and closed his eyes. High above him a Rook flew across the light blue, tinged-with-pink evening sky. Its cry hung on the air: *Ca-a-aw, ca-a-aw.* In his shuttered head Sergeant Watt pictured the solitary Rook slicing the sky; he pictured the pink-lined clouds and the first faint shades of night clawing their way up the sky's far eastern edge. Then, as he watched, the most curious thing happened. The night suddenly spurted across the sky – like dark ink dropped into a pool of clear water. And the cry of the Rook seemed to change, to become imperious and demanding. *Te-e-ell! Te-e-ell!* it seemed to say. He opened his eyes and there in front of him, exactly where they had been before going indoors, sat Tom and Jenny. 'Tell! Tell!' they cried, exactly as before. He tried to protest that it was too late, that he was too tired, but they would hear no excuse. 'Tell! Tell!' He had no choice. The rules of the game were clear: when something was unexplained, and together they cried 'Tell! Tell!!', he had to tell. So he did. Reluctantly, uncertainly, and with a strange sense of somehow being cheated, he told.

'Well . . .' he said (wondering where he should begin; then surprising himself by embarking on a lecture on the nature of history), '. . . well, the history of the world is a story of conflict, of the struggle for dominion – one species against another, one force against another . . .' (yes, true enough, he thought, but so what?) '. . . and in that struggle there have been many ages when one or another power has dominated the world and claimed it for its own. For example, there was the Ice Age, when the forces of the frozen north stormed south across the earth. There was the Age of the Prehistoric Monsters, when Tyrannosaurus ruled and it was OK to be a Dinosaur, but rotten to be anything else – well, you probably know all that . . .' (Jenny nodding confidently, Tom less so, but not wanting to appear unknowing, Sergeant Watt still secretly in the same boat as Tom.) '. . . But what you may not know – what very few people *do* know – is that once there was very nearly a Dark Age . . .' (Blank looks from both children; Sergeant Watt getting out of Tom's boat and into one of his own.) '. . . The Prince of Darkness rebelled against the light. He wasn't content with his bit of time. He wanted more. He wanted all. He looked at the evil he managed to work in the few hours allotted to him and reasoned that if all time were his, there would be no end to his achievements. So he resolved to put out the light and to put an end to all that half-baked happiness that went with it. When *he* ruled there would be no dawn and so no need for a dawn chorus; no summer sun and hence no call for flowers to bloom; no spring-time; no harvest; nothing but a long, long winter's night of cold and misery . . .' (Jenny shuddered at the thought and drew closer to her uncle. He felt himself becoming caught up in the current of the story. The struggle of the Swallows against the dark – yes, that had possibilities. But where did his helmet come in? He had no idea. He just had to trust that it would bob up somewhere downstream. He crossed his fingers and pulled on his oars.) '. . . The Prince was delighted with the prospect. And such was the zeal of his followers that his power spread like wild fire. Night by night, darkness advanced. In no time at all the whole northern half of the world was in his grasp; and whenever a day came to its end creatures drew together and prayed that it might not be their last.

Of all creatures it was the migrants who suffered most, and of them it was the Swallows, the heralds of summer, whose plight was the sorriest. Their home was in England; and though they left it every autumn to travel to southern Africa, it was almost as though they did so only to have the pleasure of returning home next year. Africa was good: it had everything they required, probably in greater abundance and of a better quality than England. But it wasn't, and never could be, their home. They could winter there happily enough, but they could never settle; and the best time of year for every Swallow was when he sensed the temperature rising to the north and knew that the annual trip to England was at hand.

So it was this year. Sensing the end of winter, Swallows from all over crammed their crops full for the annual celebration and hurried to the royal palace in the Drakensbergs. Once there they clustered under eaves, jostled on battlements, hung precariously from walls; and as the King and his beautiful daughter, Princess Hiro, bade farewell to the chief heralds, the chirping and chattering was such that the King might as well have saved his breath, for no-one could hear a word he said. But nobody cared: they all knew it by heart anyway. It was the same every year: 'Wish I could come with you. Did I tell you of the time I flew with the heralds? Yes, of course I did. Well, tell them we won't be far behind you.' Nobody heard, but everybody knew. And they knew too, as Princess Hiro smiled shyly at them, that they would fly there and back for another glance from her deep, beautiful eyes. The trumpeters raised their beaks and tweetered a fanfare. It echoed round the hillside for a second, and then the air was filled with a thunderous flutter of wings as the heralds, hundreds of them, sleek and shiny, soared up into the sky, circled twice over the palace and, borne on their way by the cheers from below, set off for the north.

Some days later, first one, then another and another battered, tattered bird flopped and hobbled its way back to the palace. And each told the same story. At first everything had gone well: they had made good progress, the wind was fair and the rising temperature drew them north as always. They flew in tight formation with no hint of the trouble to come until they were over the tropical rain forest, when suddenly everything changed: the temperature ahead dropped, the sky darkened and their fair wind was chased off by vicious cold blasts which seemed to leap up out of the forest to bar their way. Some birds had been trapped by the winds and sucked into the forest; others had been blown away east and west and were now missing, presumed dead; and the few who made their way back south were shattered wrecks, wind-shocked and broken.

The news spread quickly through the colony and once again birds hurried to the palace. But this time there were no celebrations and no festive chatter. The birds huddled in groups and wondered what was going on. What could it be? What could they do about it? Was there another route to England? Apparently not, for the survivors reported that they had tried to fly round without success – the dark and the cold, it seemed, were everywhere. What then? Must they stay here in the south – banished from their home? The thought was more than any Swallow could bear. England was home. But what was more, it was their breeding-ground – they had no other. And if they didn't get back there the race of Swallows would die. That was what faced them with the approaching dark – a sentence of death in exile – and there was nothing they could do about it.

Despair washed over them and robbed them of the power to talk, to act, to think constructively. Even feeding seemed pointless – why eat, if it meant only to prolong your agony? As though by one accord they took to their nests and lay there awaiting the end. Not even the royal palace was immune, for there Princess Hiro grieved with a sorrow the greater because it was for others rather than herself. She seemed to take the nation's misery on herself and to sink under it. She lay on her bed speaking to no-one. Her feathers lost their sheen, her flesh shrank on her frail bones. The doctors diagnosed that she was willing herself to death. But to the King, who sat by the hour at her side and gazed deep down into those grieving eyes, it was clear that she was willing others to life.

He prayed that she might have her wish. He prayed too that she might not have to die for it. And, as if prayer were not enough, he summoned his council to advise him. But they sat in silence, heads bowed – for what advice could they give? Swallows relied on the warmth to draw them northwards, and there was no warmth. The dark and cold had always been their enemies, and the Swallows' defence had been to flee until those enemies got fed up and withdrew to their strongholds. But this time they were not withdrawing: they were advancing and there was nowhere left for the Swallows to go. After sitting for hours in silence the meeting broke up with no result other than the issuing of a proclamation appealing to any bird who had a plan to bring it without delay to the palace; and saying that if the plan were adopted the author would be suitably rewarded. Then the councillors went back to their nests and the King returned to his daughter's bedside. He looked sadly down at her, stroked her limp feathers, and prayed that someone, somewhere might have an answer.

# 2

# Swallow Comes To Court

A long way away from the palace – so far that he was almost in another world – the small Swallow went about his business pretty much as usual. There seemed no reason for him to do otherwise. He had heard about the Swallows lost on the trip north, and something about the coming of the dark, and that the Princess had been taken ill. He was sorry for that, for like all the others he loved Princess Hiro: you had to, she was so beautiful and so good. He'd seen her once, when she visited his province. He had been right at the back of the crowd, craning to get a glimpse around or over two great fat females, who kept waving their wings and fluttering their flight feathers all over the place. He'd received two black eyes and severely bruised ribs for his pains. But once – just once – he'd had a clear sight of the Princess. His eye caught hers and she smiled. Not at him. She didn't smile at him. She smiled at his predicament. But for the little Swallow that was enough, and now he had only to close his eyes to see that smile again. Yes, he loved Princess Hiro. But affairs at the palace, matters of state, the flight of the heralds? They were all a million miles away. When all the big, important Swallows had flown off for the festivities, they'd left him behind to mind the barn. His job (and he'd been reminded of it often enough) was to do as he was told and not to bother himself with things that didn't concern him. And being an easy-going sort of bird that was what he did. Until he read the proclamation:

THE PRINCESS HIRO APPEAL
FOR THE DEFEAT OF THE FORCES OF
DARKNESS.

CAN *YOU* HELP?
THE NATION IS IN DANGER! OUR PRINCESS IS DYING!
Any bird coming up with a plan to defeat the forces of darkness should bring it without delay to the palace.
ALL SUGGESTIONS WELCOME

Swallow read no more for his mind was in a whirl. What was this? The royal councillors asking his advice? The Princess ill and the royal physicians seeking his counsel? Well – times had certainly changed. Then what was he waiting for? If he was to save the Princess, how could he do it stuck out here in the country? He must go at once to the palace. Without a second thought, without even going back to tidy the barn before he left (and heedless of the wrath that would inevitably come down on him), he flexed his muscles, gave his feathers the once-over, and flew east as fast as his little wings would carry him.

On arrival, so pre-occupied was he with in getting to the King, that he flew straight past the guard at the palace door, just as he was about to ask him his business. The guard turned and chased after him. He flew past the footbirds in the entrance hall and they too dropped what they were doing and followed him up the Grand Staircase. He flew through antechambers full of courtiers, who didn't even see him because he was so small, but who followed after the others (because being courtiers they could always sniff out where they should be – even if they had no idea what to do when they got there). And finally he flew past the waiting gentlebirds and landed breathless, but with quite a following, at the foot of the throne.

Guards rushed out to grab him, and the gentlebirds muttered their disapproval. But the King quietened them with a glance, and turning to the little Swallow asked him what he wanted.

'I've come . . . in answer to . . . to the proclamation,' he panted.

The King's eyes lit up. 'You have a plan to defeat the Prince of Darkness and save Princess Hiro? Then tell it – quickly.'

Now that posed a bit of a problem for the little bird, for up to now all his thoughts had been taken up with getting there. As to what to do to avert the catastrophe, it must be confessed, he had no idea – only a conviction that something must be done. He said the first thing that came into his head.

'I will go to England. I will defeat the Prince of Darkness and get to England.'

The Councillors, who had found nothing to laugh at since the crisis first blew up, put their heads back and chirped.

'Whee, whee,' they cried, 'he'll go to England. He'll defeat the Prince of Darkness. Whee, whee – now why didn't we think of that?'

But the King didn't laugh. 'Yes, why didn't you?' he asked, and the Councillors subsided.

He turned to the little bird: 'And what makes you think that you can get to England when the bravest of our nation have tried and failed?'

The little Swallow thought very hard. 'Well,' he said at last, 'I'm so small the Prince of Darkness probably won't notice me. Even if he does he won't think it worth his while trying to stop me. If all our bravest birds go together that gives him something to crush; but I won't make much of a triumph for him. And then, if I get to England, I'll have proved it can be done – despite the cold and the dark – and if *I* can do it, anyone can.'

The Chief Councillor chipped in: 'And how do you propose to find your way? We rely on the temperature to guide us and now it's cold up there. What will you do about that?'

'I don't know. I only know I'll try. And if I fail you'll have lost nothing. No-one will miss me.'

'What reward do you ask?' the King inquired.

'Reward?'

'The proclamation promised that you should be suitably rewarded.'

'Oh – did it?'

'Yes.'

'Oh. I don't know what reward. I . . . I . . . just want to save Princess Hiro – that's all.'

The King was moved almost to tears by the loyalty of the little bird. He turned to his councillors: 'This is the kind of advisor I need. Not one who counsels wisdom and shakes his head; but one who will try things which should never be tried. Go, Swallow, go to England. Make your attempt. If you fail, I'm afraid we shall see you and hear of you no more. But if you succeed, as I pray you do, I promise you as reward the wing of my daughter, Princess Hiro, in marriage – for you alone will have proved worthy of her.'

'No, your Majesty! No, you can't do that,' the little bird protested. 'I'm only an ordinary little Swallow, very young and very foolish; and perhaps it's because I'm foolish that I offer to do this, because I don't realise how silly I'm being. The Princess must marry only the best and that's certainly not me.'

'Shall we let the Princess decide?' said the King, and sent two of his attendants to bring her into the audience chamber. A few moments later they returned, carrying the Princess on a litter. They put her down next to her father and he told her Swallow's proposal.

The little bird hopped from foot to foot and turned red as a Robin from embarrassment. When the King had finished, he asked what reward she thought would befit such bravery.

She looked up at Swallow and smiled at him, a faint, weak smile that hardly touched her face, but that filled her eyes. Swallow's legs turned to jelly. Then she turned to her father: 'Bravery like that is above reward, Father. But if any bird is ready to venture so much for others, it behoves us all to love him, and in so doing to love what is best in ourselves. I could never reward him, Father; but nor could he ever stop me loving him.'

The effort of speaking exhausted her. She fell back on her pillow, her head turned towards Swallow, her eyes trying to focus on him.

'You have said well, my child,' said the King. 'Come here, Swallow.' He beckoned to the little bird to come across. 'Take the Princess's wing. All my life I have been surrounded by flatterers. They tell me how much they love and admire me, but when I need them, they are struck dumb and stand idle. But you have offered me hope: more than that – you have offered your life. I accept your offer; and in return I promise that if you succeed you shall marry my daughter and inherit the kingdom. Now kiss her to seal the bargain, and then be on your way – for there is not a moment to lose.'

Despite the King's instruction, Swallow stood at a loss. He couldn't kiss a Princess – he couldn't – not him. It was a dream. He was just an ordinary little . . . he'd only come to see if he could . . . honestly, he'd never meant . . .

'Go on,' said the King, gently; and Swallow timidly, shyly, placed his beak to the Princess's cheek. He held it there a second, while she reached out with her wing and with all her little strength held him silently to her. Then she lost consciousness. Swallow stood up.

'Now go,' said the King, 'and luck go with you.'

And Swallow, bowled over by the experience, thought that luck was the last thing he needed. He was ten feet tall and ready for anything. He bowed his way from the royal presence, out of the palace and on his way – to England.

# 3

# In The Orange Lands

Well, not quite to England. He was so bowled over by what had just happened, that without thinking what he was doing, he headed off for Australia. And who knows, perhaps he would have got there, if the other birds hadn't stopped him and pointed him in the right direction. He huffed a bit to cover his embarrassment: 'Ah ... yes ... er ... just, erm ... just practising ...' He gave his feathers a quick preen, to prove that he knew what he was talking about, shook himself and said: 'Yes ... that seems to be all in order. Right – off we go.'

And up he flew: up and away to the north.

The sun shone and the country over which he flew made him wonder whether this whole story of the approaching dark wasn't just that – a story. Everything he saw was so – so right – so beautiful – so full of life, that it was hard to believe that it was at its last gasp. Could it be true that soon the Sun would shine no more on these mountains? That the flower-covered hillsides would soon be stripped bare? The proud handsome trees stand as gaunt skeletons in a dark, dead landscape? Swallow found that very hard to imagine: yet, that was what they had said would happen, and they should know. But all he knew was that, for the moment, flying was fun. Soon it was even better for after he'd been travelling a couple of hours he crossed the border into the Orangelands. And there the wide, open grasslands and flower-covered mountains gave way to a sea of orange. Orange trees grew everywhere, their beacon-like fruit bathing the countryside in warm amber light.

Swallow had heard about the Orangelands – indeed he'd flown over them many times before, but always with the others; and flying like that, there was no way that he could stop to see whether they really were as good as everyone said. But now, on his own, what was there to stop him? Only his conscience: the thought that he should be getting on as fast as he could. Yes, but he had to rest somewhere – why not here? – and then fly on ever so much faster afterwards? Well . . . it wasn't really time yet for a rest. All right then . . . he wouldn't actually stop – just fly a bit lower to see what it was like. Yes, there could be no harm in that.

So Swallow convinced himself, and swooped down low over the tree-tops. And that was his undoing. For when he was still some way up, and while the trees still prevented him seeing what was going on, his ears were assailed by the high-pitched sounds of games and laughter. And he knew, without being told, that the sound he was hearing was that of the Orangemen – the Princes of Laughter, the closest earthly kin to the Lord of Light. He also knew that having heard them, his resolution of only looking, not stopping, was about to be broken. The laughter was so infectious that, even as he flew he found himself giggling; and before he knew what was happening, he had dipped down between the trees into an orange grove of particular brilliance.

He was still getting his breath, when he was greeted from both sides. 'Hello, Swallow.' 'Hello, Swallow.' He looked round and saw two identical orange faces.

'Hello,' he said, 'who are you?'

'More or Less,' one of the faces replied.

'Ditto,' added the other.

'I'm sorry?' said Swallow, thinking that he'd misunderstood.

'Don't mention it,' they said together and stood there beaming at him.

'I didn't quite catch your names.'

'Butterfingers,' said the first.

'You'll have to learn to catch,' added the second. 'Can't have you in the side, if you can't catch.' And they both fell about giggling. Swallow did too, although he had no idea why.

Eventually the laughter subsided and they smiled at each other in silence. It was beginning to seem that this might go on for ever, when the first one had an idea: 'Could pretend he wasn't ready and give him them again.'

'Oh yes – let's,' agreed his friend.

The first one extended his hand to Swallow: 'Allow me to introduce myself – More or Less.'

'Ditto,' added the other, likewise offering his hand for shaking.

Still at a loss, Swallow accepted the greetings, and they now felt free to explain.

'I'm More and he's Less.'

'Unless I'm More – and then he's Less.'

'They called us Orange Major and Orange Minor, you see, when we were born . . .'

'But as that's a bit of a mouthful, we shortened it to More and Less – and then forgot which was which . . .'

'And as we're both the same, no-one's ever been able to tell us. So we've both been More or Less ever since . . .'

Swallow must have looked perplexed, because the second one hastened to add: 'But we always stick together, and both answer to either name, so it's only a problem if you want to make it one.' He changed the subject. 'Have you come to play?'

Swallow was glad of the change, and was about to say that no, he couldn't play, when More (he'd decided to assume that the one on his left was always More – it made it easier) prevented him.

'Could play Hunt the Orange,' he suggested.

'Oh yes – that's a good one,' said Less.

More plucked an orange from the nearest tree and explained with an air of great seriousness: 'You see this?'

'Yes.'

'Well, you close your eyes and we hide it.'

Less completed the explanation: 'And when we say "Ready" you open your eyes and look for it.'

They were standing in the middle of a grove of twenty or more trees, each covered with hundreds, if not thousands of oranges – all identical. Swallow looked at the orange, at the trees. And then at More and Less: 'I find *that* orange – out of all *those*?'

'Yes.'

'That's a pretty silly sort of game – it'll take all day.'

'It's a very good sort of game – that's what it's supposed to do.'

'Well, I'm not playing it,' said Swallow, 'and besides I have to . . .'

'All right, all right,' chipped in Less, before he could say what he had to.

'All right, we'll play More or Less tick. That's another good one.'

'What's More or Less tick?' Swallow asked.

More told him. 'You're "it"; and you have to catch Less; but the less you catch the more you're "it".'

'What if I catch More?'

'Obviously, you're still "it", because you should have caught Less.'

'Then I'm always "it",' said Swallow.

'That's it,' they giggled. And despite himself, Swallow did too. And despite themselves, the surrounding trees did too. And despite themselves, the small, fleecy clouds in the sky did too: they held their sides and shook till they shed tears of laughter. And above them all, and despite himself, the Sun smiled too, as much as to say that from his distance he could see that they were really being very silly, but even so he could not keep quite a straight face. And when a small cloud passed across his face he was very thankful for the opportunity to splutter in secret behind it.

Eventually Swallow regained sufficient control to say that he was not going to play that game either, which caused Less to comment, somewhat sulkily, that Swallow was not much of a games player. Both he and More then began to look a little dejected and Swallow regretted that he had been so abrupt. But he needn't have bothered, for Less soon had another idea.

'I know, I know – More or Less Musical Chairs.'

'Ooh yes,' said More.

Swallow had a pretty good idea what that would involve, but asked just the same.

'Well,' explained Less, 'we walk round to the music, and when it stops we all try to sit down.'

More completed it for him: 'And the one who sits is out.'

Swallow felt bound to ask, 'Then why try to sit?'

'Can't help yourself, can you? It's a reflex. Got to be on your toes for this one. More's always getting caught out, aren't you?'

More indicated that the game was indeed something of a challenge to him, but Swallow now managed to tell them that he had not come to play games; that he was heading for England and had just dropped in to say hello. Less clapped his hand over Swallow's beak and told him to save it till he left – that way he might stay longer, and anyway it was more fun at the end.

But More was worried: 'Heading for England? Don't you know it's all dark up there?'

Swallow said that he did know, and that was why he was going.

Less too now looked at him curiously: 'I thought you Swallows were supposed to like the light?'

'We do.'

'Then why are you flying off into the dark? Plenty of light here.'

Swallow told them his story: of the massacre of the heralds on the spring migration ('Yes we got wind of that,' nodded More); of the gloom which had seized the nation; of the dying Princess and of his mission. They shook their heads at his rashness: 'Sooner you than us.'

Swallow wondered if they knew any more than he did. 'The Prince of Darkness, you mean?'

They indicated that he was precisely the gentleman they had in mind.

'Is he very bad?'

'*Bad*? I should say so. Wouldn't you, More?'

'Oh yes, he's bad all right. But more than that, he's – he's mean and – well, he's *dark*, I suppose. That's the only word for it. You never know where he is, or when he'll attack.'

'Or who his agents are. They're all over the place – even your best friend might be working for him.'

'You'd do much better to bring your Princess here. We'll look after her.'

'But won't he attack you too, if he isn't defeated?'

'He'd like to, but he can't – not in his usual way. You see, the one thing he doesn't like doing is tackling an enemy head on – he prefers to take them unawares. He hides in shadows and chooses his own moment to pounce. But here, you see, there's so much light, from so many sources, that there are no shadows – nowhere for him to hide. If he's going to defeat us, it'll have to be face to face, and he won't risk that until he's forced to.'

'Besides,' Less lowered his voice to a whisper, 'we've got a secret weapon. Should I tell him, More?'

'Yes, go on. Tell him.'

'Magic orange seeds.'

'What?'

'Magic orange seeds. Wherever you scatter them, great bright orange trees spring up and drive out the dark. So, even if he managed to force his way in here, we could still blind him with these.'

Swallow told his friends that he must still head for England, since it wasn't only light that his Princess needed, it was her home. Without that, both she and all the other Swallows would die. 'Besides' – and here he surprised himself with his own boldness – 'Dark and Evil must not be allowed to roam unchecked. Those who love the light have got to make a stand; and that's what I am going to do.'

Seeing he was not to be detained, More and Less said they were sad to see him go – it was always a shame to lose a player (even such a bad one as Swallow) – and wished him well. And Less thrust into the feathers of his breast pocket a handful of magic orange seeds. 'You never know, they might come in handy,' he said.

More too had a thought: 'He might hear news of the Tangerines.'

'Oh yes,' said Less, 'I forgot about that.'

'Tangerines?'

More explained that the Tangerines were their northern cousins, who had settled on the shores of the Mediterranean and had made that sea for centuries past a centre of light and civilisation. But it had been some time since they had last heard from them, and they feared that they might have been overrun, taken prisoner, massacred even by the forces of darkness.

Less nodded in agreement: 'If you hear of them, or can help them at all, we'd be ever so grateful.'

Swallow promised to do what he could. And then, unable to put off the moment any longer, they all finally said 'Hello' and Swallow flew off up into the orange sky.

They stood and watched him on his way, and when Swallow heard the strains of 'Here we go round the orange tree' he knew that a game of More or Less Musical Chairs was under way. He looked back as the music stopped to see More teetering on the verge of sitting down. He stayed up by the skin of his teeth; the music started up again, and they both fell on each other's shoulders, giggling uncontrollably.

High above them the Sun, Swallow, sky and clouds giggled too. And like ripples made by a stone dropping into a pool of water, the laughter in the air washed Swallow up and away, and More and Less were lost from view.

# 4

# Swallow Finds a Friend

As Swallow had heard it, the heralds had had a clear flight until they reached the rain forests of central Africa. But if that was so, the power of the Prince of Darkness had advanced a bit since then; for long before Swallow reached the forests the temperature began to play tricks on him. One moment it would be as expected and he would fly confidently northwards; the next it would suddenly drop and his confidence would plummet with it. He found it hard to say why it should so affect him. He had never bothered to think about his method of navigation before. All he knew was that if he flew with the Sun passing over him from right to left and the temperature rising up ahead, then it was spring and he was on his way to England; and if the Sun passed over from left to right, that meant it was autumn and he must be heading for Africa. But if the temperature ahead of him fell, then he was either travelling in the wrong direction or at the wrong time, and the confusion that followed was staggering. Like the heralds before him, Swallow was bewildered: his mind and his sensations were at war within him. His mind was telling him to go on but his feelings were insisting something was wrong. He no longer knew what time of day it was, or which season. He was forever stopping and starting, taking new bearings and re-assuring himself that he was on the right course. He realised that to carry on like this was to invite disaster; he'd end up as a crack-brained little bird buzzing about the countryside looking for England over each ridge, round every corner. The temperature had been his guide. But that had failed him; so he must look for another.

This now became his main concern. He scoured the countryside below for any creature who might tell him of landmarks and point him in the right direction. But for ages he saw nothing but Giraffes and Elephants, and it was useless talking to either of them, for one never remembers and the other never forgets, and neither can give a simple answer to a simple question. Giraffes were so dozy that they'd forget the question long before they'd thought of the answer. And the Elephant, well, he would certainly know. But then he knew so much (and would insist on telling it) – of the kinds of trees to be met with on the way; the precise heights of the mountains; what plants flourished at what altitude and season; what to eat and what to avoid and so on – that a bird of limited intelligence like Swallow would end up more confused than when he started.

No, what Swallow wanted was someone down-to-earth and practical.

Below him, the countryside was changing. Ever since he had left the Orangelands behind he had been flying over high, open plains dotted with characteristic acacia and baobab trees: an even, unbroken landscape that looked as though it had lain undisturbed for centuries. But now the land seemed to be suffering from some pustular disease: fresh pimples and old craters peppered the ground as though a chemical reaction were taking place just below the surface, causing countless small eruptions to scar the face of the land. He flew closer. A notice stood by the side of one of the mounds:

COPPER MINES – KEEP OUT!!!

Of course! The famous Zambesi Copper Mines! Well, if these were the mines, he should be able to find a miner or two and they could be just the sort of hard-headed creatures to help him sort out his problem.

Ignoring the notice, he flew on into the earthworks, looking for some sign of a miner. And it wasn't long before he came upon an old Aardvark scrabbling laboriously away at the bottom of one of the more recent diggings. He failed to notice when Swallow landed behind him on the rim of the crater.

Swallow coughed to attract his attention – without success.

He coughed again: this time louder.

The Aardvark stopped his work and lifted his head. He looked, or rather he sniffed around for his tiny blinking eyes didn't seem to register a great deal, but it wasn't long before his nose smelt Swallow out and gave him the once-over.

'Who are you?' he grunted.

Swallow told him. The Aardvark wasn't impressed. 'What d'you want wi' me?'

'I was hoping you might help me,' said Swallow.

'Help yourself. I'm busy.' He resumed his digging, having apparently decided the Swallow wasn't dangerous.

Swallow thought that perhaps he had chosen the wrong creature to ask. But still he would try again: 'What are you digging for?'

The Aardvark slowly raised his snout from his task and turned to Swallow. 'I am a miner in the Zambesi Copper Mines. What d'you think I'm digging for – potatoes?'

No, Swallow hadn't thought that.

''Course you 'adn't. You dig for potatoes in potato mines – everyone knows that. And in copper mines you dig for . . . ?'

'Coppers?' Swallow ventured.

'Exactly – coppers. Policemen, *Polizei*, bobbies, flatfeet, *gendarmes*, bluebottles, bogeys – whatever you like to call 'em. That's what you dig for in copper mines. And if I don't get on I won't make up me quota. It's a hard seam to work is this – I haven't struck a bootlace or a helmet all day.'

Swallow was convinced that all that digging had addled the poor miner's brain. 'You don't dig up policemen,' he said.

'Oh, don't you? Then what do you do with them?'

This Swallow wasn't so sure of: 'Erm . . . they . . . erm, just grow.'

'Like cabbages?'

'Well, no, not like cabbages.'

'Ever seen a baby policeman?'

Swallow had to admit that he hadn't.

'There you are then. Don't talk about something you know nothing about. I'll have you know you're addressing the champion copper miner of southern Africa. In one week last year I unearthed three french *gendarmes*, six London policemen, and two *carabinieri* – not to mention a couple of parking wardens and a dog handler. Got the Cup for that. Aye – they were good days, those. Not any more though – not wi' ground like this.'

Swallow was still unconvinced: 'If that's true – how do you get them to England, or wherever they have to go?'

'Pigeon post, of course: they carry them up on the spring migration.'

The Aardvark had had enough. He turned back to his work. But Swallow hadn't finished: 'There: I knew you were lying. How could a little Pigeon carry a great big policeman?'

'He couldn't,' was the answer, 'and he doesn't have to. They're only little policemen when I dig 'em up. They grow when they get where they're going.' He put an end to the conversation by turning back to his digging and burying his nose and paws in the ground.

Swallow had never heard such nonsense. True, he didn't know quite where policemen did come from, and he had never seen a baby policeman. But one thing he was sure of – they were not dug up out of mines in Africa and flown in by pigeon post. There was no doubt about it, the Aardvark's nose was not the only soft part of his head. He would leave him to his task and seek advice elsewhere.

He took off and flew up the side of the mound opposite. He was just clearing the top when something glinting in the soil at the foot of the mound caught his eye. He flew down to investigate. From ground level it was invisible and he thought he must have imagined it. But as soon as he flew back up and looked down, there it was again, as plain as a pikestaff. He called over. 'I think I may have found something.'

'If it's your way out – take it, don't talk about it.'

Swallow ignored the rudeness. 'Come over here.'

With much grumbling the old miner again forsook his digging and trundled across. Swallow pointed to the object in question. 'There,' he said.

'Where?' The Aardvark peered short-sightedly at the ground. Swallow pointed his nose in the right direction.

'What?' He sniffed it over, suddenly excited. 'Oh yes . . . yes . . . could be on to something here.' And he started to clear the earth away.

Now that he had a specific object to attack, his work rate doubled. The soil was soon piled in mounds on either side, and Swallow's beak dropped open in wonder as there emerged from the ground first the boots, then the trousers, the jacket, head and finally the helmet of a perfectly-formed, little London policeman.

'There,' said the miner, dusting him down. 'Now d'you believe me? One copper ready for delivery. Better give 'im a name. What d'you think?'

'Yes,' said Swallow not really hearing the question. But the miner took him at his word and so 'Watt' it was.

(Sergeant Watt uncrossed his fingers and smiled – so that was how he got into the story! He'd been starting to get worried. Now he could relax. He continued his story . . .)

The miner produced an oil can from his pack and oiled Watt's joints, exercised his arms in all the standard police gestures, turned his head this way and that, and then left him to continue exercising on his own, while he turned back to Swallow. 'Bit o' luck your droppin' in like that. I could've missed 'im and 'e's a little beauty, isn't 'e?'

Swallow agreed that, as policemen went, he looked pretty good.

'More'n good,' replied the miner, smiling indulgently at his discovery. ''E's champion. Look at the way 'e's got them gestures off already. There's some of 'em never gets it flowin' easy like that . . .' He suddenly broke off and pointed at Watt. 'Look! Look!'

Swallow looked. Watt in his turn was pointing his finger fiercely at something. Swallow followed the direction of the finger, but saw nothing.

'What's he doing?'

The Aardvark motioned him to be silent, and watched his little protégé agog. Watt, from pointing at this non-existent object, now held his hand upright and forbidding in front of it. He waited a moment, before lowering his hand and walking slowly, deliberately towards the object of his attention. He then bent down and seemed to be saying something to someone.

The miner glowed with parental pride. He turned to Swallow and said, ''E were practising.'

Swallow looked and was puzzled. The miner explained: 'You know 'ow some o' you birds are born with your song already in your heads, ready to come out when required – no teachin' needed – only practice?'

'Yes.'

'Same wi' 'im. 'E's born with a model of certain situations in 'is 'ead, so 'e can practise and perfect 'em like. Then when 'e gets to London (or wherever it is 'e's goin') all 'e's got to do is adapt.'

'I see... What was he practising there?'

'Routine traffic situation. Probably saw someone overshoot a traffic light; so 'e's stopped 'em 'n 'ad a word. But it's the way 'e did it – perfect, text book stuff – full o' grace and authority. 'E'll not go far wrong.'

He seemed to decide that that was enough cooing over Watt and changed the subject. 'Sorry I was a bit huffy before. It...' (he indicated the diggings around him) '... it gets you like that. The name's Alfred, by the way.' He extended a dirty paw, which Swallow shook. 'Did you say something about wanting help?'

Swallow explained about his trip to England, his problem with navigation and his need of a guide.

'Take 'im,' said Alfred, again indicating Watt, who was now executing a strange knee-bending exercise.

'How would that help?'

''E's got directions to Piccadilly Circus imprinted on 'is brain. You can't go wrong. Perfect arrangement: it'll 'elp you and save on postage.'

Swallow looked doubtful.

'Go on,' urged Alfred, ''e'll see you right, 'e will. 'Ow d'you think the pigeons got their reputations as homers, eh? Not by themselves, you can be sure of that – fat lazy lumps. No, they learn it all from my little policemen . . . That's the one thing I've got against 'em – they're ungrateful sorts o' birds. A bit o' credit – that's all I ask . . .'

Swallow agreed that it was mean of the pigeons. But Alfred shrugged it off. 'Oh, it's the way 'o th' world . . . and it's a good arrangement by and large. Anyway – like I say – 'e'll do you. Go over and get to know 'im.'

Swallow went across and said hello to Watt, to which the little fellow replied 'Hello, hello, hello' in a most curious way and followed it with another of his strange knee-bends. It was all Swallow could do to stop himself laughing. Alfred saw this and warned him that he mustn't laugh. However curious Watt's antics might be, policemen – even baby ones – didn't take kindly to being laughed at. Swallow bit his tongue and promised to do his best; and thought to himself that, quite apart from showing the way, Watt's presence would mean that the journey would never be dull. He thanked Alfred for his help, then suggested to Watt that if they were going to England, it was time they were on their way.

'Ready when you are, Squire,' replied Watt, pulling himself together; by which Swallow took him to mean that he was ready to go, though who this 'Squire' was he couldn't guess, there being no-one around but himself and Alfred, and Alfred certainly didn't look like a 'Squire'. Anyway before he had time to pursue the matter, Watt made his meaning abundantly clear by leaping lightly and unexpectedly onto his back like a knight onto his charger. Also like the knight he dug his heels into Swallow's sides (which Swallow could well have done without), patted his neck (which he could likewise have dispensed with), turned his head to the north, waved farewell to Alfred and, before Swallow knew what had hit him, they were on their way.

Swallow made a note to have a word with Watt, when the time was right, about his riding manners; if they were to get on he must insist on being treated more like a friend and less like a police horse. Otherwise, the next thing you knew, he'd be getting lumps of sugar stuffed into his beak.

No sooner had they cleared the northern edge of the mines than the soil at the bottom of some long abandoned workings bubbled briefly. A small shadow slid out and headed silently northwards. The soil fell back into place as though it had never been disturbed.

# 5

# In the Tropical Rain Forest

Navigation was now the easiest thing in the world. Swallow just flew; and every so often Watt would yell 'This way' or 'That way' (or more disturbingly 'Gee up', which confused them both since neither knew what it meant). And despite the fact that the temperature continued to be erratic, they made excellent progress. Flying was again a pleasure; and Swallow smiled as he thought how silly the heralds had been not to get themselves a guide like Watt. But then they were probably too busy being heraldic – or whatever heralds were – to think of anything so practical.

And down below him the African landscape smiled too; a sun-drenched countryside, stretching endlessly out beneath a cloudless sky, spotted only by the moving freckles of two shadows – theirs and another.

After they'd been flying for some time a great mountain range began to form on the horizon ahead of them. Gradually the land became more hilly and then they were in amongst the mountains and Swallow had to climb and zig-zag to find his way through. Watt grew very impatient at these detours. He seemed to think the mountains had no right to be there and, whenever they were heading up a valley which was not in precisely the right direction, he would cry imperiously, 'That way! That way!' as like as not pointing straight at a rock-face which towered above them.

Swallow soon learnt to ignore him and fly on, confident in the knowledge that at the end of the detour Watt would still be there shouting, 'That way!' But even if they avoided the highest of the peaks and the worst of the climbs, the effort still took it out of Swallow; and no sooner had the smile come back to Watt's face as they breasted the last ridge and swooped down into the last valley, then Swallow began to look around for somewhere to rest and get his breath back.

To his surprise he spotted a place at once. They were just about to fly out of the mouth of the valley, when down below them and framed at that moment in shadow he saw a sign-post which marked the crossing of four tracks.

'Just the job' he thought, and flew down to it.

However it turned out to be no ordinary sign-post, and it was far from providing the quiet place-to-get-his-breath-back that Swallow had sought. From the moment he settled on one of the fingers Swallow knew – and with a strange sense of foreboding – that he had made a mistake. His feet itched uncomfortably so that he couldn't keep still. And, although the Sun was shining on them, both he and Watt shivered uncontrollably. Swallow put this down partly to the cool of the evening and the extraordinary exertion of flying over the mountains; but more – it was because he had a feeling of being watched, over-looked, pointed out by some hostile power; as though the fingers of the sign-post had turned and instead of pointing away down the four tracks were now pointing back at him.

There was no staying here. Tired as he was, Swallow determined to fly on and find somewhere else to rest. He took Watt again onto his back and flew up and away. But just as they were about to clear the end of the valley and to emerge into the open air, a violent cross-wind sprang up from nowhere, knocked them sideways and carried them back down to deposit them once more on the post. Then the wind vanished and all was calm, silent and still. The shadows lengthened in the evening sun.

Swallow shivered. His feet itched. His flesh clustered in bunches on his bones. Again he flew up. Again he was about to break out into the free air outside the valley, when the wind barged into them and hustled them back.

And again Swallow shivered in the Sun. But now there was no trace of cold in the shiver. Now it was all fear. What was going on? Who was doing this to them and why? He tried to collect his thoughts, which were spraying wildly round the valley looking for enemies behind every tree, under every rock, and to get them into some sort of order. First, the sign-post had attracted them – they hadn't even had to look for it, it had just presented itself the moment it was required. So they had flown down to it. Now it repelled them. It made them so uncomfortable that they couldn't rest; yet when they tried to move on, the wind barred their way. Why? They had been brought here and now they were being kept here. *Why?*

Was there something down here they were meant to do? To see? Something which they couldn't see from their perch on the sign-post? Was it – whatever it was – on the sign-post? The directions? Was he to read the directions and follow one of the paths? The shadows creeping across the valley seemed to nod 'Yes' in agreement, and though Swallow recognised this as only a trick of the light, he had no doubt that he was right – that was what was wanted of him. Yet he was reluctant to comply. He sensed an evil mind at work and wanted nothing to do with it.

He tried once more to spear his way through to the air outside. Once more the wind ambushed him and sent him cartwheeling back down; and he knew that he had no choice. The mistake had been made when they flew down into the valley. Now that they were there, he must read the directions, or they would never get out. This time he let the wind carry them past the fingers and put them down on the ground at the foot of the post, and there was no itching.

Watt got off and stood by his side. They glanced briefly at each other and then, as if by mutual consent, they looked up and read the directions.

Swallow's suspicions were confirmed. There could be no doubt – the sign-post was the work of the Prince of Darkness.

There were five fingers on it – one to each point of the compass and one more pointing up into the sky. This last said 'OUT OF BOUNDS' and Swallow already had proof that that meant exactly what it said. But what to make of the others? These read in turn 'OUT OF TIME', 'OUT OF YOUR DEPTH', 'OUT OF THE QUESTION', and 'OUT OF YOUR WAY'.

What on earth could they mean?

Obviously they were 'in' something (trouble most likely) and the sign-post offered a choice of ways out. But whether out and on their way, or simply into more and deeper trouble, Swallow couldn't say.

He stared at them as if hoping to squeeze out their meaning; and at last he did manage to make some sense of the first, which pointed back the way they had come. If they didn't get to England, time would indeed run out for the Swallows down south. But as to the others, he found them all pretty unpromising, and almost all equally baffling – though for some reason that he couldn't explain, he felt that they should choose the last and go 'out of their way'.

He turned to Watt to see if he had any ideas, and Watt had no hesitation in pointing to the way 'OUT OF THE QUESTION'.

'How d'you know?' asked Swallow.

'Easy,' Watt replied. 'You asked me which way we should go, and I answered, "That way", so that's the way: "OUT OF THE QUESTION".'

Swallow knew Watt should be right. He remembered Alfred's words – ''E's got directions to Piccadilly Circus imprinted on 'is brain – you can't go wrong' – but he wasn't sure.

He *should* trust Watt – but he couldn't. He didn't know why, but he felt that the path 'OUT OF THE QUESTION' was not right.

He told Watt so and suggested that they might do better to go 'out of their way'. But this the little policeman refused point-blank to do; and when Swallow continued to press the point, he turned on his heel and strode off down the path of his choice.

Still Swallow hesitated, fearful to commit himself. But he knew deep down that the decision had been made for him: they must stick together. So when Watt reached a bend in the path and was about to disappear from view, Swallow stifled his doubts and flew after him.

The path went down and down, becoming narrower and darker with every step of the way. At first a mantle of trees covered the path, filtering the light and providing just the conditions in which the dark liked to stretch itself. Then that canopy was itself blotted out by a dense network of smaller trees and creepers which closed over them, and the few shafts of light which penetrated to them now were weak and frightened. They seemed to have strayed in by accident and were now wishing they could get out again.

Which was pretty much how Swallow felt too. He raced to catch up with Watt, partly to raise again the question of their going a different way, but also because he didn't want to be on his own: this forest gave him the creeps.

Eventually he came level with Watt and with great difficulty persuaded him to stop: 'Watt . . . Watt . . . wait a minute . . .'

Watt paused impatiently.

'I don't care what you say – this is not the right path. I think we should turn round and go back to the crossroads.'

'Turn round if you like,' said Watt, and proceeded to do so, 'but there's no going back. Look.'

Swallow looked behind him and saw to his horror that the path they had come along had completely disappeared: behind them the jungle had closed in.

He gave a start and drew back closer to Watt. The creepers seemed to reach out, to beckon him. The tendrils groped towards him. And he heard a voice from the blackness of the jungle whisper: 'Come to me, Swallow. This way, Swallow.'

He clung to Watt. 'Listen,' he said.

The voice repeated: 'This way, Swallow.'

'What is it?' Watt asked.

'Listen!' said Swallow again.

'I'm with you always, Swallow,' came the voice from the shadows. 'You can't lose me, not while the Sun shines. And then, when the Sun doesn't shine . . . ha ha ha ha ha ha . . .' It ended in a low chuckle.

Swallow froze. His tongue stuck to the roof of his mouth. For a moment he lost the power of speech. Then the fit passed and he turned to Watt: 'Did you hear that?'

Watt looked at him puzzled: 'Hear what?'

'That voice. The voice coming out of the jungle.'

'No, I didn't hear anything. Only the wind in the creepers.'

'Are you sure?'

''Course. If there'd been a voice, I'd have heard it. It was the wind.'

Swallow listened again and now he too heard only the wind.

Watt continued with a wisdom far beyond his tender age: 'It's the imagination that does it. You'll hear all sorts of things in the jungle if you listen to your imagination.' He watched Swallow sympathetically, seeming to reflect on the awesome power of imagination over those who were in its thrall. He smiled, counting himself fortunate not to be prey to it, then went on: 'Still, I don't suppose you'll want to go back that way any more?'

'No,' said Swallow, 'no, we'd better go on. But quickly. Let's get out of here as quick as we can.'

'Roger. Wilco,' said Watt. 'Over and out.'

Swallow, tricked again by Watt's habit of addressing third parties, looked over his shoulder for Roger Wilco, but saw no-one, only the groping creepers. And when he turned back, Watt had vanished. Swallow stared around him in panic. Where had he gone? 'Watt! Watt!'

Then, tapped out under the jungle noises, he heard Watt's footsteps echoing down the path. He hurried after them.

*

The further they went the darker it got, until it was so cold and dark that Swallow was covered in goose pimples and could hardly see his beak in front of his face. He travelled on guided only by Watt's footsteps up ahead, which now in the depths of the jungle sounded hollow and strangely rhythmic. And elusive; try as he might he couldn't catch up with them.

He began to wish that he'd never volunteered for this task. He wasn't a hero – he should have known. Only big birds are heroes. Swallows should stick together and keep out of the way. 'Stupid bird,' he thought, 'stupid, stupid bird!'

He flew faster, fearful that the creepers were coming after him. He felt them snatching at his tail and called out involuntarily, 'Watt! Watt!' and swerved to the side into more creepers which clawed his face.

He veered away violently into a tree trunk, smashing his wing against it and drawing blood. Winded, he collapsed into the crevice at the base of one of the branches and cowered there, his eyes staring blindly into the darkness, tears streaming down his cheeks, sure that at any moment the creepers would get him. 'Watt! Watt!'

Frozen with terror in his cranny, it seemed to Swallow that the tree had suddenly become alive: it was crawling with enemies. He could chart their progress. They were moving in from the edges, creeping along the branches towards him.

His heart pounded, like a Woodpecker trapped in his breast, trying to get out; and keeping pace with his heart, he could hear Watt's footsteps, faster now, but still no nearer, no further away, tantalisingly out of reach.

'Watt! Watt!'

The enemies inched towards him. One, on the branch above, had reached the treetrunk and was now groping its way down. Swallow heard it slither on the damp trunk. Then silence, before it sent one of its tendrils whipping like a strand of spider's web, across his face.

He thrashed the thing away and hurtled in panic from his perch.

Heedless now of the path, he careered ever deeper into the jungle, a small, self-propelled dart smashing his way through leaves and creepers, past trees and tendrils.

'Watt! Watt! Wait for me!'

His cry echoed round the jungle and was repeated on all sides – 'Wait . . . Watt, wait . . . for me . . . Wait! . . . Wait . . .' – until in his fevered imagination it seemed that it was the jungle calling to him – 'Wait! . . . Wait! . . . This way, Swallow . . . Wait for me . . . I'm with you always, Swallow . . . wait for me . . .'

Swallow flew like a bird possessed. He flew as no Swallow had ever flown before. He didn't know where. He didn't care. Everything was wiped from his brain but the need to escape his pursuers, and the conviction that somehow Watt represented sanctuary. But where was Watt? Why could he never get any nearer? Why would those footsteps never stop? What was wrong – surely he must have heard?

He wanted to cry out again, but feared that the pursuers would again take up the cry. So in sheer, blind panic he flew through the black depths of the forest. He flew further and faster than he would have believed possible and long, long after his strength was spent. He flew and flew until he crashed head on into a huge mahogany tree. He crumpled like a concertina, hung there impaled for a second, then collapsed unconscious to the ground.

'Bull's eye,' hissed the voice, and a sycophantic giggle rippled round the clearing.

Watt, alarmed for his friend, struggled to get free, but every movement served only to wrap him more tightly in the coils.

'Keep still,' hissed his captor and squeezed him so that he thought his head would burst and his brains plop out like sauce from a bottle.

'See that the bird's all right,' the voice went on; and from all sides birds of brilliant plumage flew down and jostled around Swallow.

When he came round, Swallow's first thought was that he must get on or the creepers would catch him. What was he doing – falling asleep, when he was in such peril? He struggled to get up, but the pain in his head made him fall back, and it was only then that his eyes began to focus on the multi-coloured canopy above him, and his ears began to register the babble that emanated from it.

'He's coming round! He's coming round!'

Slowly the outlines sharpened and the words separated and were recognisable; and he saw to his relief that he was surrounded by birds – all sorts, all beautiful, and all looking down at him with studiously solicitous faces. For the first time since entering the forest Swallow felt almost safe.

Then the canopy parted; the faces turned away, crying exultantly: 'He's all right! He's all right!' And Swallow found himself looking up the tree, up into the sinister smiling eyes of the Black Mamba – Lord of the tropical rain forest, Viceroy to the Prince of Darkness.

The hope, so newly planted, withered in his breast.

He looked again at the birds who had greeted him and recognised them now as those birds, famous in proverbs, who had sold their birthright in exchange for gorgeous liveries: Grey Parrots, Babblers, Whydahs, Fly-catchers. Their story was told by every mother Swallow to her nestlings to keep them from similar folly. They had once been ordinary birds like Swallow, but had longed to be beautiful and, unable to satisfy that yearning in the sunlight, had agreed to give up the freedom of the air and become servants of darkness and of the Mamba. And now, sad and resplendent, they paraded in their borrowed liveries before their master – a constant witness to the power of dark over light.

Swallow saw Watt too; and why it was he had never been able to catch up with the footsteps. They were not footsteps at all, not really. Watt hung enmeshed upside down in the Mamba's coils, while the great snake's tail flicked first one foot then the other against the trunk of the tree.

And Swallow saw that his flight had been for, and from, nothing. He had fled from the dark into the dark – his every move dictated, controlled by his enemy. And he saw for the first time, in something like its true scale, the size of the task he had taken on.

The Mamba's green eyes glinted venomously, lighting up

the clearing and colouring everything in it. He lay in the tree, perfectly still and perfectly black except for the eyes which, like balls of green fire, rotated independently of each other and surveyed the whole arena, paralysing anything on which they fixed.

'Welcome to my palace,' he hissed. 'We've been expecting you.'

His courtiers laughed as though he had said the funniest thing in the world. He allowed this to go on for a second, then turned his left eye lazily upon them. They fell silent.

His right eye remained fixed on Swallow. It bored into him, seeming to shrink him with its glare: 'Well,' he demanded, 'aren't you going to say something?'

It was a moment before Swallow could think to speak. Then he stammered out, 'W-w-w-w-what are you doing with Watt?'

'What?'

'Yes – what are you doing with him?'

'Who?'

'Watt.'

'No, not what; who,' corrected the Mamba.

'Him – Watt,' said Swallow pointing. 'My friend.'

'Oh, *him*,' the Mamba smiled. 'Just hugging him.' He gave Watt another squeeze. Watt's face went purple. The Mamba turned him upright and flicked out a caressing tongue. 'Dear little fellow.'

Watt ducked back into the coils, only to pop out again in response to another squeeze. His face was now as black as the Mamba, with fury.

'Put him down,' said Swallow.

'Oh, I don't think I could any more. I've grown attached to him.'

The Babblers gurgled their delight: 'He's grown attached to him, he's grown attached to him.'

The Mamba continued to flick Watt with his tongue, producing always the same response – flick, duck, squeeze, pop – flick, duck, squeeze, pop. It acquired a rhythm of its own and the assembled birds chirrupped in time.

Then the Mamba seemed to tire of the game and said sadly, 'But alas – I suppose he has rather outlived his usefulness . . .'

He rolled his left eye back to fix it again on Swallow and, as he did so, a glinting green tear fell from the glinting green eye, as though the eye itself were melting with the pity of it all. Swallow shrank away from the teardrop, fearful that its touch might poison him.

The Mamba went on: 'I'll tell you what I'll do. If you agree to serve me, then I will let him go.'

'No,' said Swallow. 'I will never serve you. And besides, if you let him go, he would die trying to get out of the jungle. You know he would.'

'Do I?' hissed the Mamba, closing one eye to squint at him; then opening it again with a malicious laugh. 'Yes, of course I do. Well then, what do you propose?'

Swallow thought for a moment, then said, 'If you let us go – both of us – then we will promise to tell everyone how good you were to us.'

'Oh, how kind,' murmured the Mamba. 'There's only one problem. I don't want you to tell everyone how *good* I am, but how *bad* I am.'

And with a sudden jerk, he uncoiled his tail and catapulted Watt away through the trees into the black jungle behind him. His courtiers went into fits of admiring laughter: 'How bad he is! How very bad he is! Isn't he bad!'

The Mamba's gaze turned again to Swallow, the smile wiped from his face, his eyes smaller now, contracted with hatred – pinpricks of intense green light which shot narrow beams of malice through Swallow.

'There. As you so rightly say, your friend will die trying to get out of the jungle. And you, Swallow, you will either serve me, or your friends the creepers will get you. Oh yes, I know all about the creepers. They're waiting, out there in the dark, waiting for the light to go out. When I go, I take the light with me. Then it's up to you. If you want to serve me, you have only to call – I shan't be far away. Otherwise . . . I shall wish the creepers joy of you.' So saying he slid gently off his perch and disappeared.

The clearing was again plunged into darkness and Swallow was back where he started: trapped, terrified in the jungle – a prey to all the enemies his imagination might conjure up.

Watt too had a problem. He was splattered against a tree.

Not from being thrown by the Mamba – he had survived that with nothing more serious than a few cuts and bruises. Being still very young, he had rather enjoyed the sensation of flying solo and then crashing helmet-first through the undergrowth. But once on his feet he had lost no time in heading north as fast as his legs would carry him.

And therein lay his dilemma: his homing instinct pulled him north like a magnet, while his feelings all told him he should be going the opposite way. He had suffered unheard-of indignities in the coils of the Mamba. Not only had he been held and hugged and squeezed, but the great, greasy, green-eyed creature had been laughing at him, and had encouraged others to do the same. Such insults had to be avenged. Besides, Swallow was back there. He had got Swallow into this mess and he couldn't just abandon him. Yet even as he thought this, his feet were carrying him further and further away. And it was only by walking into the great tree which loomed up in his path, that he had given himself a moment's pause. But already his instinct was edging him round the tree and he knew that if he didn't think of something soon, he would be on his way again, Swallow would be lost, and the Mamba's insults forever unavenged.

Further south Swallow lay in a sweat. The jungle had come alive again. It was just a matter of time before the creepers got him, and when they did the only question was whether he would die on the spot, or die later for the shame of crying out for the Mamba. Then suddenly he thought of the magic orange seeds and kicked himself for not thinking of them before. They would drive off the creepers, surely? He reached down for them, then hesitated. Wouldn't they also bring back the Mamba? And then where would he be – his secret revealed, his allies betrayed, his destination perhaps made plain – and yet no further forward? No: the orange seeds were not the answer – not yet. Reluctantly he withdrew his wing and edged as close as he could to the tree. He lay there, not daring to move lest someone should notice.

The creepers moved in on him. They were everywhere. They rustled on the ground on either side – now here, now there, never staying in one spot long enough for him to focus on them. They swept across him, breathed on his face, whispered in his ear, 'And then, when the Sun doesn't shine . . . ?'

Rigid with fear, bathed in sweat, Swallow could hardly breathe. Desperately he thought – could he serve the Mamba? Would it matter if his name became proverbial for treachery as the Babblers' and Whydahs' had done? They survived. They had their beautiful feathers, which were all they had wanted. Mightn't he do the same? Swallow saw behind their laughter and chatter to the secret sadness of birds who would never see the Sun, whose beauty could only ever be revealed in the light of their master's eyes. He knew that for him such a life would be no life; but even so, wouldn't it be better than this shivering shame on the forest floor?

He thought blushingly back to the scene with the King – the trust that had been placed in him. He had been so bold then, so brave, and now look at him! He thought of Princess Hiro, of her smile, her wing round his neck – yet look at him! Was he a fit champion for a Princess? When all that had been offered could not spur him to one moment's dignity, let alone heroism? A wave of self-disgust welled up inside him and he answered his own question. No, he was not fit; he was fit for nothing, good for nothing but to serve the Mamba and so by his own wretched example to show others what not to be – he must become, like the Babblers and Whydahs, an object lesson in unworthiness. 'Mamba,' he cried.

A single green eye appeared at once above him and fixed him with its narrow beam. The suddenness startled him: he had supposed the Mamba to have moved away. 'Well?'

Faced again by his adversary, Swallow had second thoughts; but he overcame them: 'I . . . will serve you.'

'I thought you might,' mocked the Mamba, looking down on him in more ways than one.

In the dark all around them an unseen audience babbled its appreciation: 'He will serve him . . . He's going to join us . . . We knew he would . . . The Swallow will join us.'

The cry was passed on through the jungle, the jubilation of the birds being augmented by the excited jabbering of Monkeys, who sensed that an event was at hand and were soon swinging through the trees to make sure of the best vantage points in the neighbouring branches.

The Mamba's second eye rolled up and turned its beam on the audience, silencing them. Then in the silence he explained: 'I'm afraid there is a little more to it than just saying you will serve me. First you must tell me that you *want* to serve me.'

'I want to serve you.'

'That you hate the light and pray that the world will be covered in darkness.'

This was harder, but Swallow thought of the light which would reveal his shame, and managed to say it: 'I hate the light and pray . . . that the world will be covered in darkness.'

The Mamba smiled: 'And that Princess Hiro – may die.'

Swallow was silent.

'Come on, Swallow – or I won't believe you. Say after me: "I pray . . ."'

Swallow forced the words out: 'I pray . . .'

'That Princess Hiro . . .'

'That Princess Hiro . . .'

'May die.'

'May . . .'

He could manage no more. Despite his resolution, despite his self-disgust, the words stuck in his throat.

'I can't. I can't say it.'

'Then I don't believe you want to serve me.'

'I do, I do. But why must I wish the Princess Hiro ill?'

'Because she represents the light in the world; and when you serve me, you will want all lights to be put out.'

'Her light will be put out. All Swallows' lights will. Cut off from their breeding grounds the race will die. Why must I wish it?'

The Mamba thought for a while and the audience discussed the proposition among themselves. 'Why should he wish it?... He should hate her... We do... Of course we do... So should he...' Again the eye glanced at them and they fell silent.

'Very well, Swallow, I accept what you say. You need not pray that the Princess will die. But one thing remains: if you are to be my servant, you must surrender your flight feathers to me...' He paused for the idea to sink in, then added, '... New feathers will then grow, which will enable you to fly where you will within the forest, but never out of it. Do you understand?'

Swallow nodded. 'Yes, I understand.'

'Good. Then stand out in front of the tree, where we can all see you, and raise your wings to me.'

Swallow did as instructed. He moved about six feet from the tree, turned, and raised his wings to the Mamba, where he lay coiled on the branch.

The chattering of the audience subsided to an expectant hush. The green eyes glittered with anticipation.

The Mamba did not move until Swallow was absolutely still and the audience absolutely silent. Then, when he was finally satisfied that not even a leaf was stirring, he began the ritual.

The two eyes concentrated their beams on Swallow and threw the surroundings once more into blackness. Swallow now stood alone in a pool of green light. Slowly the eyes moved towards him, as the Mamba's head and upper portions must have slid down the trunk and out in his direction. They stopped inches from his face. The voice taunted him: 'You still have time to change your mind, Swallow. The creepers are waiting...'

Swallow did not flinch.

The Mamba smiled, then swayed silently over to Swallow's right wing. The mouth opened to seize the foremost flight feather. Saliva dropped from the fangs. Swallow closed his eyes and braced himself for loss of feather and freedom.

But the mouth never closed. Instead it opened wide, wider – it gaped open in rage or astonishment and sent out a fierce guttural hiss, which all but blew Swallow off his feet.

He opened his eyes to see the head jerk over to its side and crack down on the ground as the rest of the long, serpentine body toppled leadenly from its perch. The eyes lost their focus and sprayed fractured green beams crazily around the clearing. Terrified courtiers fluttered, shrieking, hither and thither. Jabbering, squeaking Monkeys danced up and down in the branches of the trees. Chaos reigned.

Swallow shrank back, imagining that his feather must have been ripped out and that this was the sensation that went with it. He instinctively drew himself in, making himself as small as possible. He heard a voice, small but authoritative: 'Let that be a lesson to you, Green-eyes. Don't you ever make fun of a policeman again!'

Watt! It was Watt!

Swallow searched for and saw him. Triumphant Watt, terrible Watt, terrific Watt, boot raised from where he had just unseated the Mamba like avenging justice in the crook of the great mahogany.

Reacting to Watt's voice, the green beams turned on him, but before they could fix him, Swallow was in the air and had smashed, beak-foremost, into the back of the Mamba's skull. Again the head cracked down on the ground and instead of seeing Watt, the Mamba glimpsed his very own green galaxy.

Swallow took his chance and flew on the instant up to the branch. Watt leapt onto his back, and they fled from the clearing.

They flew in the dark, but Swallow was no longer afraid. Watt's presence and a strange exhilaration at having temporarily seen off the Mamba banished his fear.

Behind them the rabble of courtiers was whipped into order and sent shrieking and crying after them. And in the dark of the jungle they would surely have caught them. They knew the jungle, were adapted to flight within its confines; they could see better, were fresher; there were many more of them. In the darkened jungle, Swallow had no chance – it was only a matter of time before he was overtaken and carried back to his enraged enemy.

But that enemy now made his second mistake (his first having been to antagonise Watt). In his fury, his eyes burning once more with full power, he turned and sent poisonous beams shooting after them through the trees.

For the first time since he entered the forest, Swallow could see where he was going. His heart leapt. The Mamba had given him the chance he needed. He had made it into a straight race between Swallow and his pursuers, and racing was the one thing Swallow knew all about.

The pursuers were at that moment close behind him, hot on his heels. He could hear the flap of their wings, smell their hot breath. Another second and they would close in. But they didn't have another second. Just as Watt was about to urge him for the umpteenth time to 'Gee up', Swallow did; and they both realised at last what Watt had all the time been talking about.

The pursuers were left gasping, grasping thin air as Swallow shot from them. Now instead of scraping past creepers and smashing into trees, Swallow swayed and swerved, swooped and soared round, past, over, under, and through obstacles with Watt riding him like a champion jockey.

The courtiers and their noise were soon left far behind and Swallow, following his and not Watt's instinct this time flew on through thinning dark to be greeted first by a few adventurous shafts of light, scattered and stray; then by others less bold but more numerous, who played among the shadows on the edges of the forest, until at last the dark was gone and they emerged into the full brilliance of the African day.

'We've done it!' cried Swallow, whooping for joy and sending Watt shooting up into the air, as from a trampoline. They danced through the air – separating, coming together, separating, coming together. And down below on the ground their shadows also danced.

A third shadow separated itself from the forest. It danced too. But not for joy.

# 6

# How Does Your Garden Grow?

They had come out on to a plateau high to the east of the forest. Free at last from fear of the Mamba, Swallow felt suddenly exhausted and desperately in need of refreshment. He looked for somewhere suitable to rest; and while he did so Watt explained how he had made his way back to the clearing and surprised them all.

'Well, I enjoyed being thrown by old green-eyes, you see.'

'Yes,' said Swallow, mystified.

'Don't you see what that means?'

Swallow didn't, but suggested that perhaps Watt would grow up to be a flying policeman. This gave Watt a vision of a future in the Flying Squad, and he glowed with premature pride. But such grandiose notions were foreign to his nature and he was quick to banish them.

'No, no. I enjoyed it. And I am programmed to travel to England. So – I must have been thrown towards England. Being thrown in any other direction would have been far from pleasant.'

Swallow agreed that this seemed to make sense, but still failed to see the relevance.

'Well, once I landed in the undergrowth, I naturally got up

and headed for England, right?'

'Yes.'

'So my journey on foot was a direct continuation of that through the air, and to get back to the clearing all I would have to do was to work my way back in exactly the opposite direction – holding on to the trees and bushes as I did so. That was what I did, and it brought me straight back to the mahogany tree. I saw that the Mamba was about to do something pretty nasty to you, so I shinned up and gave him the boot, so to speak.'

Swallow was dumbfounded, and said so.

'Oh, it's nothing – just routine detective work.' Watt tried to pass it off as something of everyday occurrence; but they both knew it was much more. It was, in fact, the first bit of real police work that Watt had been called on to do, and he had performed it with distinction. He could not suppress his excitement, and began at once to look for new challenges to his developing powers. He was not long in finding one. 'Let's go down there,' he cried.

The land below had undergone a gradual and magical transformation. Irregular outcrops of rock gave way to gently rolling slopes; brown, straggly grass changed into close-cropped lawn; isolated, hard-living trees gathered into well-fed, contented clusters. Imperceptibly, the wild African landscape had merged into a beautiful garden, and they now looked down on what seemed to be its focal point: a natural spring of silver water, which bubbled up and then ran sparkling through grass so green it was like a bed of emeralds, and banks of flowers which glittered as a dozen treasure chests.

But it was not these that had attracted Watt's attention. What interested him was the vast concourse of animals which jostled each other by the stream, milling around and vying for position like guests at a garden fête – Elephant, Giraffe, Gnu, Gazelle, Wildebeest, Water-buffalo, Zebra, – every animal you could mention and all in a muddle. Watt recognised it at once for what it was not: just the sort of situation he was made for. He saw chaos; and hurried down as a bringer of order.

No sooner had Swallow touched down, than Watt was off into the middle of the mêlée. A shrill blast on his whistle commanded attention; and then, with the authority of his cloth and quite regardless of the size of those he was ordering about, he took control. Like a matador in a bull-ring he mesmerised the animals. He stood there, proud and provocative. His arms twirled in complex flamenco gestures, luring the animals forward, spurring them on to a high pace. Then, when they were passing him at full gallop, he would raise a peremptory hand in their faces and bring them crunching and bumping to a halt. At the same moment he would pirouette away with a coquettish, come-hither gesture and bring other animals into the action.

Each signal communicated immediately to the animal traffic. They moved forward, veered away to the left, swung to the right, stopped, backed, waited and surged, all in obedience to their miniature master. Those who before had milled more or less aimlessly, and more or less happily, were miraculously sorted into neat rows: Zebras heading one way, Lions another, Elephants another and so on; all in files, all under his control and all absolutely stationary.

Watt surveyed his handiwork with pride: perfect order – not an animal out of place; and not an animal moving to spoil the pattern. Perfect.

Watt smiled: he felt ready for London.

Swallow meanwhile had gone over to the stream for a drink. He settled down some way above Watt's traffic jam, not far from the spring, and opposite a large boulder on which was perched a small, red-billed bird – a red-billed Ox-pecker, Swallow thought.

The bird was staring angrily into the water and when Swallow nodded 'Good day' to it, it either did not notice, or could not be bothered to return the greeting. So, seeing no-one else around to interrupt his refreshment, Swallow bobbed his beak into the stream and drank.

Nature, however, had trained him to keep his eyes open when drinking; and he saw the whole scene – garden, river-bank, boulder, bird and himself – all reflected in the water.

He also saw the boulder move. He saw the side which had been covered by the water rise ponderously up into the air and cast a dark shadow over him. He saw it lurch out over the stream and seem to be about to flatten him into the darkened water. He leapt back out of reach of the shadow, up onto the sunlit bank; and there – from a safe distance – he looked again.

He found himself staring at the huge horn, round spectacles and weather-beaten grey face of an old Rhinoceros gardener. Water dripped from the battered features, giving him a very sorry appearance. He held a newly-filled watering can in his mouth, which also dripped.

Swallow stared at him; and he stared back at Swallow, but he seemed not to see him. All his attention was taken by the little red-billed Ox-pecker perched on his back who, the moment his head appeared out of the water, let fly at him. 'Call yourself a gardener!' she cried. 'Call yourself a gardener! You've let those Elephants make a meal out of your baobabs. *And* they've ruined the lawn. They come tramping all over it with their great feet, without so much as a by-your-leave and you let them!'

The Rhino ventured to say that he couldn't stop them, even if he wanted to. The garden was there for everyone.

'Everyone except me! They eat your grass. They chew your trees. And you say nothing. But when I ask you for something, when I ask you to grow me a few flowers – you can't do it! Won't do it, more like. I mean – look at it. It's pitiful!' She turned and pointed to a flower bed which, in contrast to the abundant vegetation all around, was indeed very pitiful. One or two shoots had poked their heads above the ground, but seemed already to regret their boldness. They stood there, limply apologising for their existence and wishing they could return whence they came. Otherwise the flower-bed was bare.

'Well, now we know where we stand, don't we?' said the Ox-pecker. 'You needn't expect me to keep you clean and tidy any more. Oh no, I've got plenty of other things to do, don't you worry. You can look after yourself for a bit and see how you like it.'

So saying, she flew off and busied herself chasing the motes in the sunbeams. The Rhino who, behind his horn-rimmed spectacles and armour-plated hide seemed to be a gentle, peaceful soul, had borne all this with the long-suffering air of one who expects to be abused. And now that his assailant had gone he muttered only, 'I'm sorry, I'm sorry,' and carried on with the forlorn task of ferrying water from stream to flower bed.

When he next returned to the stream, Swallow whispered across, 'What's the trouble?'

The Rhino looked all about him, trying to locate the voice.

'Over here,' whispered Swallow.

The Rhino blinked behind his spectacles at him. 'Oh, you've made it!' he exclaimed in surprise.

This was not at all the response Swallow had expected. 'M-m-m-made what?' he stammered.

'You're arrived,' said the Rhino. 'Oh, that *is* good news. I thought we'd lost you when you went "out of the question".'

'H-h-h-how did *you* know about that?' Swallow asked, casting his mind back to the sign-post and remembering the feeling he'd had there of being over-looked.

'Heard it on the grape-vine, old boy. I was rather banking on your coming 'out of your way' to help me; because, quite frankly, I need all the help I can get. But then I heard you'd gone the . . . the other way and thought that meant the end of the road for you and a lifetime of old worry-guts for me.' He indicated the busy little bird, who was bustling about dusting anything she set eyes on – anything that didn't move – which, of course, now included Watt and the traffic-jammed animals.

The Rhino turned again to Swallow. 'I must say, I am glad you've proved me wrong.'

'I wanted to come this way,' said Swallow, then pointed to Watt and added, 'but he said the other way was quicker.'

'More direct, yes. Quicker, no. As the Crow flies, that is the most direct route. The only trouble is that Crows don't fly very often round here, because they've all been caught by the Mamba – which is why I thought you were a goner, when you went off that way . . . But anyway you weren't; and here you are; and now there's hope for both of us. Here . . .'

He broke off to fumble down his side, as though searching for ticks. Swallow pretended not to notice. Then the Rhino turned back to him and there in his hoof, presumably from somc pocket hidden among the folds of flesh, lay an assortment of seeds. He held them out to Swallow: 'Ever seen anything like these?'

Swallow hadn't. He was not an expert on seeds. In nine cases out of ten he couldn't tell one from another. And so it was now. The seeds all looked pretty much the same to him and he had no idea what they were. Only one or two – a tightly-knit cone, and a bone-hard shell with the seed presumably locked somewhere inside it – seemed vaguely familiar. Not that he knew even them – he didn't. But he had heard of seeds rather like that, which depended on fire to wake them up. Anyway that was all he could think of.

While he was thinking, the Rhino continued: 'Her cousin – one of the yellow-billed Ox-peckers – gave her these and told her they had the most delightful flowers and she was to get me to grow them for her. So I planted them; and I covered them with Giraffe manure – the best of its kind; and I've watered them every day with water straight out of the spring over there, which should make anything grow. But – as you see . . .' He gazed ruefully at the unforthcoming flower bed, seeming to hold it personally responsible for all his misery. 'I suspect it's a trick – I wouldn't put it past the yellow-billed one – an attempt to make me look silly and to prove that I can't even garden properly. But if so, she's succeeded, because I'm blest if I know the answer.'

Swallow's hunch had been right – he was sure of it. The seeds must all depend in one way or another on fire to get them going. 'You'll have to burn them,' he said.

Rhino looked at him as though he were mad. 'Burn them?'

Swallow nodded.

Rhino heaved a sigh. 'I've often wanted to, I can tell you. But she'd make my life a misery if I did.'

'No, burning makes them grow. At least, it might – it does with some flowers. I think it will with these. Go on – quick – while she's dusting Watt.'

'What?'

'My friend – the policeman. Watt's his name. She won't be finished with him in a hurry.'

They considered for a moment the spectacle of Watt who, at the touch of the Ox-pecker's feather duster, had begun to dance like a dust-devil. He was not quite the docile, dustable object she had expected. Swallow went on: 'She's so busy, she won't notice the fire. All she'll see is the flowers beginning to grow.'

Rhino was still doubtful. But on Swallow's repeated urging, he thought he might as well give it a try. He had told Swallow that the little Ox-pecker would make his life a misery if he burnt the seeds – but on reflection he realised that, as she did so already, he really had nothing to lose. He left his can on the bank and trotted over to the flower bed. There he scraped together a bundle of dry leaves and some old Giraffe manure, over which in time-honoured Rhino fashion, he rubbed two sticks together, and in no time at all the flower bed was happily ablaze.

They stood back and watched the flames dance over the ground and, as Swallow had predicted, the Ox-pecker, absorbed in Watt, was busily unaware of the inferno behind her. And would have remained so, but for one thing. Swallow had reckoned without Watt's fire-fighting instinct.

At the first whiff of smoke, Watt froze. He forgot the feather duster; he forgot the traffic; and he concentrated exclusively on this new hazard. The trumpetings of the traffic-jammed animals all around him went unheeded as he sniffed the breeze and, his eyes lighting on the blazing seed bed, tore towards it with whistle blowing and arms waving.

'Fire! Fire! Come on now – keep clear! Stand back! Come along, we don't want anyone getting hurt! Let the Dog see the Rabbit! Watch out for falling masonry! Women and children first!'

The words tumbled out of him: a torrent of expressions

which neither Watt himself, nor anyone else present had ever heard. None of them knew the meaning of the words, but Watt instinctively realised they were the right sort of things to say in this new and frightening situation.

And they certainly worked, though not quite perhaps in the way he intended, for they alerted the little red-billed one to the imminent death of her flowers. Never had Swallow seen so small a bird so full of fury. Her beak seemed to glow even redder with rage. She flew at Rhino and hurled insults at him, accusing him of destroying the flowers just to spite her.

'Good-for-nothing . . . Incompetent . . . Shiftless . . . Ne'er-do-well . . .' A fusillade of abuse flew about Rhino's ears. He closed his eyes, sank his head into his shoulders and waited for the storm to pass.

Swallow tried to explain that the whole thing had been his idea and that if she were to wait a little, she might see what they were up to. But Swallows have never been very good at making themselves heard – he felt like a fly shouting at a thunder storm. There seemed to be nothing for it but to wait – as Rhino was doing.

Then Watt again intervened. 'Well, well, well,' he said, giving one of his curious knee-bends. 'What have we here?'

They turned to him. He was standing by the flower bed, where the fire had now run its course. The old, sorry shoots had gone; and in their place, healthy young green shoots were appearing everywhere. They bubbled up like springs of underground water. And they grew like magic, as though having been shut up for so long, they were now determined to make up for lost time.

They popped out; stood up and stretched themselves; spread their leaves and smiled. Plants of all shapes and sizes: small fat round ones; long tall thin ones; squat and spiky ones; big and bristly ones. And the flowers – red and yellow; purple; pink, blue and orange and scarlet – a patchwork rainbow. They stood there looking around them, nodding to each other as much as to say, 'Oh – you're here too. Good to be out, isn't it?'

But more amazing than all, the Ox-pecker, for the first time in her little life, was struck dumb. She opened her mouth to speak, but the words wouldn't come. You see, she'd never tried to apologise before and now that she wanted to, she found she didn't know how. And maybe she never will, for Rhino put her out of her misery, saying, 'That's all right, dear. I hope you like them.'

And with his big Rhino hanky, he ever so gently wiped a tear from her eye, as she said, 'They're beautiful, dear – quite beautiful.'

To hide his embarrassment, Swallow bobbed his beak back into the stream to complete his interrupted drink. Then he turned to Watt and said, 'I suppose we'd better be on our way.'

Rhino begged them to stay. 'Don't go – please. You don't have to go, do you?'

'Do you?' echoed the Ox-pecker.

'Do you?' echoed the shade of the acacia tree, mockingly, but nobody heard it.

Swallow thought how lovely it would be to stay; but even as he thought it, the image of his dying Princess came to him and he said, 'I'm afraid so. I have to defeat the Prince of Darkness and get to England. Besides it would be a pity to waste all that effort getting past the Mamba, only to stop here.'

Still Rhino tried to dissuade them, but when Swallow pointed out that Watt could not be detained and that for himself, he was bound to go where Watt went, then Rhino abandoned his efforts and said, 'Well, at least let me give you something to take with you.'

He produced a little bottle and filled it with water. Then he corked the bottle and handed it to Swallow. 'This is magic water. It comes from a secret spring, far below the earth's surface and, if collected, as this has been, before it touches the ground, it is proof against the powers of darkness.'

Swallow held the little bottle up to the light and it was so clear that it was like looking into the source of light itself, as though all the clearness and brilliance of sunlight had been collected and refined down to its ultimate purity. It shot rays in all directions over the garden. The shadows under the trees were taken by surprise. They shrank away into their secret places. One of them hissed malevolently.

Rhino went on: 'If you are to get to England, you will need protection. That water will cure you of any ills put on you by the Prince of Darkness. While it lasts, he will not destroy you.'

'Thank you,' said Swallow, and put the bottle into his pocket next to the orange seeds. The shadows under the trees reverted to normal.

The little Ox-pecker was showing signs of agitation. She kept hopping about, muttering something about the Sage of the Sahara.

'I'm coming to that,' said Rhino gently, and the Ox-pecker subsided. 'When you come to the Sahara,' he explained, 'there is both good and bad in store for you. The bad is that the Prince of Darkness will send the Wild Wind to blow you off course.'

'And the good?'

'The good is that if you look hard, you will meet the Sage of the Sahara. And you must meet him, for he alone can help you to defeat the Prince of Darkness.'

'The Sage of the Sahara?'

'Yes.'

'Yes,' whispered the shadows, 'the Sage of the Sahara.' And one of them slipped unnoticed away.

'What does he look like?' asked Swallow.

'Can't say,' answered Rhino. 'He's all things to all creatures. The only time I ever met him, he was a Scorpion that I'd just decided not to stand on. But I doubt if he'll look like that to you. But don't worry – you'll know when you've seen him. And if he feels that someone is really looking for him and needs his help, he'll find a way to get to them. The Wild Wind will do everything he can to chase you out of his kingdom, but you must wait for the Sage of the Sahara.'

*The Sage of the Sahara.* Watt inscribed the name in his notebook; then returned the book to his breast pocket and expressed his readiness to depart. Swallow thanked Rhino and Ox-pecker for their help and, after many good wishes on the one side and hopes one day to return on the other, he and Watt took one last look at the newly-released flowers swaying in the breeze, and with that hopeful image in their minds set off once more on their way.

# 7

# Stuck in the Sahara

Watt plotted a course north by north west to take them smack across the Sahara.

Time passed. The garden vanished as it had appeared – as if by magic. Swallow might have doubted whether it had ever existed were it not for the little bottle which nestled in his pocket. And after the garden, the brilliant sunlight went too and they flew on into a deep red, suffocating sunset. The air was heavy with dust. It made their eyes smart and caused them both to cough and catch their breath.

Time passed. Below them on the ground the trees became fewer, the grass sparser, the vegetation scrubbier and scrubbier, until it was no more and then, when they looked down they saw only sand. Sand everywhere. The sands of the Sahara, stretching away as far as the eye could see; and the further they flew, the more sand appeared.

But at least there was no sign of the Wild Wind; and they could concentrate instead on looking for their promised helper, the Sage of the Sahara. They scoured every inch of the waste below looking for... looking for... Well, what were they looking for? Neither of them knew. Something that moved. *Anything* that moved. Anything. But there was nothing. No sign of life.

Time passed. Still they flew and still sand unrolled below, sometimes flat and low, sometimes hilly, mountainous even. But always sand, always desert, always rejecting the Sun's advances, and always remaining cold at heart however scorching the surface.

When they had started into the desert, fresh from the garden, it had seemed to Swallow that the end really wasn't too far away. After all, he had already travelled from the south of the continent; and across the Sahara could only be the same again. No, that didn't seem too far. But the further they went, the further the end receded, until it seemed quite possible that there would be no end, except theirs – their death in the desert.

With memories of the mistake they had made in going 'out of the question', Swallow wondered whether they should go back and try to find a way round. But, as earlier, Watt was immovable; and anyway, Swallow could himself produce two convincing arguments against such a move: they had still to meet the Sage of the Sahara, and there was no knowing whether it was further to go back or to go on. So they went on.

Their eyes were like running sores; they poured gritty tears in a continuous stream down their cheeks. They longed to close them, if only for a second, but they remembered Rhino's words: 'If you look hard, you will meet the Sage of the Sahara.'

And they did look hard. Despite the dust, despite the pain, despite the longing of their eyes to close and shut out the endless red roller-coaster which sped past beneath them, they looked. They looked until Watt no longer saw a red desert, but a sea, with mountainous waves rolling past one after another; and there on the crest of the next wave, bobbing helplessly, was a small fishing-boat. He blinked and looked again. It was still there and it was in distress. The sailors called to him, 'Help! Help!'

Swallow saw something too, but not quite what Watt saw; perhaps he wasn't looking in the same direction. He saw a great stetch of water fringed with rich, heavy palm trees. Rhino and Aardvark dozed peacefully under the trees, while Lion, Zebra and Giraffe paddled in the water. Like Watt he looked again to make sure he wasn't seeing things; then called out, 'Do you see what I see?'

'Yes, come on. Let's get down there.'

They flew down. But the moment they got below the sky-line, fishing-boat and oasis disappeared. Watt feared that the boat had gone under; but Swallow knew that distances could be deceptive in the desert. Things would seem to be almost within reach, when in fact they were many miles away.

So up they flew again, and there on the crest of the next wave, Watt saw the fishing boat bobbing and heard the sailors calling; and Swallow saw again the palm trees leaning over to canopy the dozing Rhinos.

Again they flew down; again boat and oasis disappeared. They breasted the next dune and there they were again; and again and again.

And so intent were they on chasing the mirages, that they didn't hear the little winds creep quietly up behind them.

Finally they flew over a dune larger than all the others and this time no fishing boat and no palm trees appeared. Instead, a great golden sand castle rose towering in their path, only a few yards away, the drawbridge lowered towards them. They turned to go back, but flew straight into those same little winds that danced around now, yapping at them, nipping their heels, herding them forward.

Swallow cursed himself. He had been so busy chasing the mirage that he'd quite forgotten about the Wild Wind. And now here they were, all but in his power. He tried to veer away to the left, to the right, but whenever he did so, there were the winds waiting for him and blowing sand into his eyes and sides, blinding him and pricking his skin till he felt like a flying pin-cushion. There was no way out. Bit by bit they were edged nearer and nearer the drawbridge until finally, despairingly, they allowed themselves to be blown across it and into the castle courtyard. The winds scurried over behind them. The portcullis fell; the drawbridge was raised; and they were caught in the castle of the Wild Wind.

Swallow had seen castles before, but never the like of this. It wasn't built, but rather blown up out of the surrounding sand. And having been blown up it was held in shape by countless gangs of slave-winds which chased continually through windows, round walls and over battlements, whipped on by the fierce gusts of their vicious wind-guards. And whenever one of them flagged, he was unceremoniously snuffed out and substituted by a fresh breeze, which slipped into place and carried on the chase.

It was a masterpiece of masonry: tower topped tower topped tower, like a giant's stairway to the sky. And at the top, where it seemed about to pierce the sky and to disappear from view, Swallow could just make out a frieze of snow-capped turrets – the icing on the Wild Wind's cake.

Yes, there was no doubting its magnificence; but what made the castle all the more impressive, to Swallow at least, was that it seemed to be constantly renewed – like a river, ever changing, ever the same – so that each glance was as the first and took one by surprise. It was as though the Wild Wind's peculiar property was to be constantly redefining himself and testing his adversaries' perceptions.

But he had other properties as well, of which the courtyard provided ample evidence – for there the Wild Wind's crack troops practised martial arts. In one corner a row of weather vanes had been erected and wind-troopers were practising with them, rushing at them full-tilt, then blowing suddenly as they passed and sending them spinning. Their accuracy was awesome.

Others trained in a sort of shooting gallery: they crouched at one end and aimed at matchstick-like targets at the other end, a hundred yards off. And not only did they hit their nominated targets – they obliterated them, while leaving their neighbours, an inch away to either side, untouched. Elsewhere a group had formed up and was battering a great door. It must have weighed a ton and looked quite impregnable. But the winds softened it up with two preparatory taps, and then, with unbelievable force, sent it crashing back on its hinges.

But most impressive of all was another group, dancing around and working themselves into a frenzy. They danced in ever decreasing circles, faster and faster until they were spinning almost on the spot. And when they reached this point it seemed that they went into a trance, for they suddenly rose up in a spiral column, up into the air and stood there swirling and swaying – a savage whirlwind.

The little winds allowed Swallow and Watt just time enough to be impressed with what they saw, before ushering them across the courtyard towards the main entrance to the citadel. Swallow had no doubt that that was the one place they should not go, that the Wild Wind was in there waiting for them, and that once inside their cause would be lost. Hoping that even now there was a chance to meet the Sage of the Sahara, he tried all he could to hang back, and willed Watt to do the same – but in vain.

Far from delaying, Watt strode ahead with such purpose that the little winds had their work cut out keeping up with him. He was hopeless! Why couldn't he think? It seemed that so long as he was heading for England he pressed on regardless, caring nothing for dangers that might lie in his way, or for help that might go begging. What was the matter with him? Had he so short a memory? Had he already forgotten the mess he had got them into (and out of) with the Mamba? And the Rhino's warning about waiting for the Sage of the Sahara? Why did Swallow always have to think for both of them? If they hung back they might stay a minute longer in the courtyard; might delay for one more minute the meeting with the Wild Wind; might give the Sage of the Sahara one more minute to reach them.

But it was not to be. Watt climbed the steps and entered the citadel; and Swallow followed, unwilling, but unable on his own to hold back for any length of time. The little winds blew the door shut and bolted it from the outside.

Swallow turned angrily to Watt. 'Now look what you've done! Why couldn't you wait?'

'What for?'

'What d'you mean, "What for?" The Sage of the Sahara, of course.'

Watt looked abashed. 'Was he there?'

'No. No, he wasn't there. But...'

'...that was where we were to meet him?'

'Well, no. But...'

'But what? There's no point waiting with all those winds around.'

'There was a chance of meeting him there. And there isn't here.'

'No chance here... No chance here...' whispered a voice behind them in the walls.

This time they both heard it, and were both afraid. They drew together and looked warily around.

They were in a dimly-lit, brick-red tubular corridor, undecorated save for a kind of irregular ribbing which projected at intervals along the walls. And, staring into the half-light, it almost seemed that the walls were moving – contracting and expanding slightly but regularly like a concertina lightly touched. But that must be the blood throbbing in their heads. There was no visible source for the voice.

Watt whispered, 'I'm sorry. It has to be something very strong for me to hang back. I managed it in the jungle because you were in trouble and the Mamba had insulted me. But I can't just wait on the off-chance. I'm sorry, I don't know how. I'm sorry.'

Swallow saw that Watt was near to tears. He turned his anger from Watt to himself. How could he blame Watt? He was still so young. He had a job to do, which he was doing well. If they got into trouble, that was Swallow's problem. He hoped, he prayed, that they might yet meet their promised helper. But he couldn't for the life of him see how.

The walls *were* moving! And what was more, Swallow and Watt were going with them. With each contraction of the walls a breath of air was summoned up from somewhere behind them; and with each expansion it blew past and edged them a little further down the corridor away from the door.

'No chance here,' whispered the voice in the walls.

The door now came to represent security. Swallow tried to go back to it, and for once Watt was prepared to go with him. But it was like walking the wrong way up an escalator – all they manged was to stay where they were, and when they stopped walking they were edged further away.

'Why was it,' Swallow wondered, 'that every time he thought of going back, something occurred to prevent him?'

'No chance,' whispered the voice.

Then, before they knew what was happening, a violent gust had appeared from nowhere, knocked them off their feet, and was hurtling them down the corridor. The voice in the walls laughed as they were bowled along: 'No chance . . . Ha ha . . .'

Down and round then went. Round and down. 'Ha ha ha . . .'

On and on. The laughter always with them. 'No chance here.'

Swallow craned his neck round to catch sight of the voice. But whichever way he turned, the voice turned too and seemed always to come from just behind him, just out of reach; and all he achieved by his efforts was a severe bruising from crashing into the projecting ribs of the corridor.

Watt too received a pretty savage battering. He, of course, bitterly resented the laughter, and he too located it directly behind himself, and no amount of twisting and turning availed to bring the scoffer into view.

Who was he anyway – this scoffer? Was that the voice of the Wild Wind? Swallow didn't think so: he didn't sound very wild – more mocking, taunting – more like the voice Swallow had heard in the jungle – not the Mamba, the other one. But if not the Wild Wind and not the Mamba, then who? And why in any case was he following them? Swallow framed the question, then at once forgot it – even unformed the answer frightened him.

Instead he concentrated on the Wild Wind. When were they going to meet him face to face? After all, that presumably was why they were here. They were in his power. When did they get to meet him?

Then he realised his mistake: the Rhino had never said they would meet the Wild Wind, only that he would do all he could to blow them off course and out of his dominions. And that was just what he was doing. They wouldn't meet him – well, not face to face at least. But they had already come into contact with him, were in contact at that very moment. Unless Swallow was very much mistaken, they were even then in his windpipe and on their way to be spewed out over the Mediterranean! And if they allowed that to happen, they would have crossed the desert without meeting the Sage of the Sahara. 'You must wait for the Sage of the Sahara.' Rhino's words rang in his head. He knew that to let the Wild Wind have his way would be to put an end to their hopes and to throw away all their efforts.

He called out to Watt, 'Try to hang on to one of the ribs.'

Now their experience in trying to locate the voice came in handy, for in order to steer out of the current and over to the sides they simply looked behind themselves until they banged into a rib, and when they did so, tried to latch onto it. They missed a few, received more bruises in the process, but at last each hooked onto one and hung there, feet and tail streaming, like flags in a force ten, downwind away from them.

Swallow told Watt the situation as he saw it: 'If we let him throw us up when and where he wants, we might as well have stayed at home. We've got to make him cough us up before he's ready.'

'How?'

'Well, if we are in his windpipe, we should be able to make our presence felt . . .' He reached down to his tail. '. . . Hang on, I've got an idea . . .' He clenched his beak and ripped out the longest tail feather he could find. 'I don't know what'll happen. So be ready.'

Watt tightened his grip.

Swallow took the feather and tickled the sides of the windpipe. At once the ribs convulsed and the wind gusted violently, all but tearing them from their moorings. He repeated the process, with the same effect. He was satisfied. 'Good. Now I'm going to tickle it once more – properly this time. It should cause a great convulsion followed by an enormous gust of wind. All we have to do is wait for the wind, let go, and trust to luck. Ready?'

'Yes.'

'Good. Here goes.'

Again Swallow tickled the sides of the windpipe and again the ribs convulsed. But this time Swallow allowed them no time for recovery, he kept on tickling and they convulsed with ever greater intensity until they cramped up completely for a second before producing the predicted gust.

'Now,' cried Swallow.

They let go and were at once propelled up the windpipe like flying phlegm, up through the throat, past tonsils, past uvula, over tongue towards teeth . . . 'Happy landings,' called Watt, straightening himself for a dive . . . between teeth and through opened lips, to be belched out bullet-like into the air.

They landed in a heap and with a bump. It was a moment or two before either of them could collect their senses sufficiently to take in their surroundings. Watt was the first to recover. He pushed his helmet back from his eyes and looked round.

They lay in the corner of an enormous wind-swept chamber. Wherever he looked he saw sand. Sand curtains hung before sand windows; a sand table was surrounded by sand chairs; and what light there was came from a sand fire which smouldered sullenly in a sand grate – smouldered that is, except when receiving the attentions of the Wind, its master, for then it perked up and flared, fawning.

The master referred to was at that moment looming over Swallow and Watt, snorting with fury and with his hand clasped in horror to his mouth, as though he had just let the cat out of the bag.

Watt needed no introduction: this was the Wild Wind. And he was tumultuous. He didn't waste his time practising skills or working himself into a frenzy like the whirlwind in the courtyard. He terrified without trying. Even at rest he measured twelve on the Beaufort Scale, and when roused he was immeasurable. And he was roused now. Savage gusts issued from his mouth, down his nostrils, out of his ears, up through his hair. Especially up through his hair, which was so furious it was quite out of control, as were his clothes. They looked likely to burst at any moment; or rather, as though they had burst several times already and were about to do so again. And his anger seemed to feed on itself, for gusts once expelled, crashed into walls or whatever else lay in their way, and rebounded, to be sucked back in again by the Wind and blown out with redoubled vigour a second later.

While Watt registered all this, Swallow too regained consciousness, aided in no small measure by the buffetting he received. And like Watt, he recognised the Wind at once, and knew what he must do: stand up to him. The Wind loved creatures who cringed and cowered. On no account must he cower. He knew that. But face to face it was hard not to.

The Wind was so big, so powerful, and he so puny. The awful disparity numbed his mind and made resistance seem pointless. If he stood up he would at once be blown down, if not blown to bits. If he shouted he wouldn't be heard. If he tried to run and hide, there was nowhere the Wind couldn't reach. Perhaps it did look like cringing, but if he kept his head down he stayed alive and while there was life... Well, perhaps there was hope.

Such complicated reasoning was beyond Watt. He saw a bully and stood up to him: 'The Wild Wind of the Sahara – that's what you call yourself, is it? Puffed-up little pipsqueak – ooh...' The Wind picked him up and hurled him the length of the table. He collapsed gasping in one of the chairs.

'...think you're pretty good out here, don't you? Surrounded by toadies who flatter you all day long... aaaagh...' He was tossed high into the air and smashed against the wall.

'...I'll have you know that in London we've got winds ten times your size sweeping the streets – ugh...' Again he smashed into the wall, his helmet knocked askew by the impact. Swallow marvelled at Watt's courage, but feared that it was suicidal.

'... If I got you... aaagh...' And again he was smashed. His helmet fell to the ground.

'... If I got you in Scotland Yard... I'd have you docile as a summer breeze... Ohhh...' And again. His eyes span in his head. '... inside two minutes... Oooooh...' And again. His legs buckled. He no longer knew where he was. Only instinct kept him going. '... You don't know you're born...' Without the Wind touching him he collapsed to the floor, still talking. '... all wind, that's what you are... all wind...'

With a viciousness that defied description the Wind picked up the sagging body and tossed it like a rag doll about the room – into table legs, against walls, under chairs. It bounced him in the air as heading practice, and still the words poured out meaningless, undirected, instinctive – nature fighting on where intellect had failed: '...allwindassoon as someone standsup to you yourefini sheddontknowwhichwayto turnandlookatyou whatdyouthinkyoulooklikeascarecrowthatswhat youareascarecrowyouareadisgracetotheforcestandupstraight shouldersbackchestoutandgetyourhaircut...'

Swallow had heard enough – more than enough. He should have stopped this long ago. What sort of coward was he to lie there, to watch his friend suffer? While there was life – perhaps there was only shame and disgrace.

He no longer thought; he no longer weighed the pros and cons; he just reached into his pocket, grabbed a handful of the magic orange seeds, and threw them with all his might at the Wild Wind.

# 8

# Look and You Shall See

A flash like a thousand fireworks blinded Swallow; and for a moment all he could see was a negative image of the stunned, open-mouthed Wind, as he had looked at the moment the seeds hit him. Then gradually his eyes adjusted to the light and the image shrank protesting to join its original behind a row of great bright orange trees, which sprang up to form a wall of light separating Swallow and Watt from the Wild Wind.

And by the light of the oranges Swallow saw. For the first time since he had glimpsed that oasis in the mirage, he saw things as they were and not as the Wind wanted him to see them.

The branches on the near side of the trees arched over to form the roof of a bright corridor, which stretched across the chamber, then continued on through where the wall had been a few moments ago. Swallow blinked. He wondered how it was he hadn't seen it before. He also wondered where the old Camel had come from who was kneeling down, tending Watt, on the floor of the corridor a few yards away.

The Camel beckoned him across. 'Come on,' he said. 'We've got to get him out of here before they recover.'

Strangely Swallow felt no need to question the Camel's authority, but moved at once to his side and lifted Watt in his wings. There was something about the Camel that inspired total trust. But there was another reason for Swallow's eager obedience. Behind the wall of light something was happening. A voice could be heard addressing the Wind: 'You were supposed to destroy them!'

'Sssssssssss...' They heard the Wind shrivel like a pricked balloon.

'I told you they were coming. I warned you, gave you every chance.'

'Sssssssss...'

'How *dare* he bring his ghastly orange light into my kingdom! Somebody will pay for this. You mark my words!'

It was the same voice! The voice Swallow had heard in the jungle; the voice they'd both heard when they entered the citadel, the voice in the wall, the voice from the shadows. The voice of the Prince of Darkness!

With Watt in his wings Swallow clambered onto the Camel's back and settled himself there, his beak clutching the fringe on top of the hump. Then the Camel rose and, seizing a branch from the nearest orange tree to light their way, sped off with long strides down the corridor. As they went Swallow heard the voice order the Wind into action! 'Get your troops here at once! And get rid of this light!'

Soon, however, they had left all that far behind and the only light in the corridor was that shed by the Camel's branch, the only sound his footsteps and their thoughts.

The moment he considered it safe, the Camel stopped, knelt down, and ordered Swallow off his back. Swallow obeyed in some fear. Had he walked into another trap? Had he trusted too much too soon? But the Camel stilled his fears by examining Watt and saying, 'You'll have to revive him quickly, or he'll die.'

'Yes,' thought Swallow, 'yes we must revive him. But how?'

The Camel seemed to read his thoughts and filled in the blank. 'Use the water Rhino gave you,' he advised. 'Wet his lips. Just a drop, mind, or he'll run amok.'

Swallow did as he was told. He reached out the little bottle, uncorked it and moistened the tip of his wing. He felt a strange and delicious tingling shoot through him. He rubbed the damp feathers over Watt's lips.

Even before the action was complete the water began its work and he felt the life course once more through the little policeman's veins. He sat back and watched with wonder as the water ran its restorative race round Watt's body. Bumps subsided, bruises lost their angry discolouration, and open wounds closed, healed and disappeared – all in a matter of seconds.

Watt stretched like one awakening from a deep sleep, yawned, blinked, sat up and looked around him. His gaze settled on the Camel.

'Who are you?' he asked.

The bluntness of the question – particularly asked of one who had so lately saved his life – shocked Swallow, and dimmed a little his delight at Watt's recovery. Still he was glad the question had been asked. It had been troubling him for some time.

'I am what I am,' replied the Camel, cryptically, and got up to go.

'And what's that?' demanded Watt, showing that he had a short way with smart repartee.

'A Camel at the moment. I should have thought that was obvious.'

'A Camel, eh?' Watt looked him up and down. 'You weren't here before.'

'Yes, I was. But you didn't see me. You were too busy believing the Wild Wind's bluster and ballyhoo. You couldn't see what was under your nose. Now come on . . .'

He started to move off, but Watt stopped him. 'Just a minute. Just a minute. What's your name?' He reached for his notebook.

'I haven't got a name . . .'

'No name, eh?' Watt raised a disbelieving eyebrow and licked the point of his pencil.

'. . . but others call me the Sage of the Sahara. Now come on, we can't waste time . . .'

'Known as the Sage of the Sah . . .' Watt never completed the entry in his notebook.

'The Sage of the Sahara,' Swallow repeated, his heart jumping for joy.

'Yes. Now put the bottle away and follow me.' He picked

up the branch and headed off down the corridor. Swallow and Watt restored bottle and notebook to their respective pockets; then Watt climbed aboard and they sped off in hot pursuit.

But they had not gone above a few hundred yards when an ear-splitting cry from Watt brought them shuddering once more to a halt.

'What on earth is it?' demanded Swallow. The little policeman clutched his head.

'For heaven's sake,' said the Camel, hurrying back, 'do you want to tell everyone where we are?'

But Watt wasn't listening: with his hands covering his head he looked about him wildly. 'My helmet! My helmet!' he cried.

'What about it?'

'Where is it?'

Swallow and the Camel stopped and looked at Watt, and sure enough – he had no helmet. They had not noticed it before. It had not been sufficiently important – not in comparison with their main purpose, which was to get out of reach of their enemies. But it was important to Watt. He was overcome with embarrassment. Like a cat without its whiskers, or a sheep newly-shorn, he felt naked and ashamed. He refused to go on without it. Swallow and Camel tried all they could to persuade him that his authority was unimpaired, that he could get another helmet in London, but it was no good. Watt crouched there, head in hands, immovable, inconsolable.

Camel whispered to Swallow that if they pretended to go, Watt might follow. Swallow agreed to give it a try. They turned to Watt and Camel said, 'We can't wait. If we stay here, we'll be captured.'

Watt didn't move.

Swallow urged, 'If we don't go on, we'll never get to England.'

Still no response. Swallow turned to Camel: 'Come on. We'll have to leave him.' They took up the orange branch and hurried off, down the corridor, round the corner and out of earshot. Then they stopped, and stood, silently praying that

Watt would follow. Several times they thought they heard him coming, and expected him to appear round the bend at any moment. But each time they were disappointed.

At last Swallow could bear it no longer. 'We'll have to go back,' he said. Camel nodded and back they went, back to the spot where they had left Watt. But Watt was no longer there.

Swallow panicked. Where was he? Why wasn't he there? Had they come to the wrong place? All sections of the corridor did look very much alike.

'Watt!' he called, 'Wa...'

Camel stopped him: 'Sssssh.'

'But what's he doing? Where can he have got to? We'll never get out of here. I know it. I know it!'

Camel calmed him down and suggested that Watt must have gone back to fetch the helmet. They would have to follow. They would soon overtake him, since he was travelling blind, while they had the orange branch to light their way. And, once re-united, Swallow could stay with Watt, while he went back to the chamber to get the helmet. 'Have you any idea where he dropped it?' he asked.

Swallow had. He pictured the whole scene: Watt being battered by the Wind, the thud of the little body against the wall, the helmet coming off. 'It's under the table,' he said. 'It rolled there during the fight.'

'Right,' said Camel, 'I'll get it.'

'No,' protested Swallow. 'They'll get you. Much better, we go back, find Watt, knock him out and carry him on with us unconscious.'

'And what will happen when he comes round? If he's this concerned about it, don't you think he'll head back from wherever you've got to? And then you'll have lost your guide and your friend. And you're going to need them both, believe me. Anyway, the Wind won't get me. He can only brow-beat creatures who see things this way – as you both did. Then, no matter how brave you are, he'll destroy you. But if you see through him, as I do, then he is as his name implies – just wind.'

'But he's not alone...' said Swallow, imagining that he was

sharing a secret.

'I know . . .' Camel read his mind and stopped him saying more. 'I'll have to take my chance with the other one . . .' His eyes glazed over for a moment as he seemed to contemplate a prospect which he too found horrifying. Then he blinked, as if to wipe it away, and went on. 'Now listen carefully, because I won't have time to say this again. If I don't get back, you are to fly down the corridor as far as you can go. Whenever there's a choice, follow your instinct – don't wait for second thoughts. First thoughts are your own, second thoughts may not be. If you do that, it will bring you at last to a corridor, at the end of which you will see a large wooden door. It will be locked. This is the key.' (He gave a key to Swallow.) 'That door marks the northern edge of the desert; beyond it lies the land of the Barbary Apes – the next stage of your journey. Go through that door; bolt it behind you; and you will be safe from the Wind at least. I can't answer for the other . . .'

Again he seemed reluctant to put a name to the Voice, as though even to utter his name was to admit his power. But Swallow knew who he meant and nodded accordingly.

Camel then produced an hour glass, which he held out to Swallow. 'Take this. You may need it. But let nobody see it or know about it. Nobody. Do you understand?'

Swallow took it, mystified. 'Not even Watt?'

'Especially not Watt. He must not even suspect its existence.'

Swallow felt this to be a betrayal of his friend, and thought that perhaps when they had gone on some way, he would find a time to let Watt into the secret. But even as he thought it Camel said sternly, 'He must not know. Not until you have reached England. Otherwise it will lose its power.'

Swallow felt abashed. 'I won't tell him. I promise.'

'Good.'

'But what is it?'

'A life-timer. Your life-timer to be exact.'

Swallow was still mystified. Camel saw his puzzlement, but paused a moment, as though wondering just how much he could afford to tell even to Swallow. Then he beckoned him to come closer and whispered in his ear, 'There is a secret desert deep in the Sahara. It is called the Time desert, and is made up of the Sands of Time. The sands of everyone's life who ever was or will be, are contained in that desert. Those in that glass come from there. They are the sands of your life.'

Swallow found the information fascinating; and, looking at the grains of sand trickling slowly through the neck of the glass, he was pleased to see that he still had a good way to go. But he couldn't quite see why Camel had chosen this moment to give him the timer, or how it would help him on his journey.

Camel continued: 'You are going to fight . . . someone' – again he refrained from naming him – '. . . and I cannot fight him for you. You must defeat him on your own, by your wit and your resolution. If he overcomes you by fair means, then you deserve to be his servant and the timer will not protect you. But, should you outwit him, and should he detain you by cheating, then if you turn the timer upside down, you will fly from his grasp and to your destination.'

He paused to allow the information to sink in, then added, 'But mind – if you use it before then, in an attempt to shorten your journey or to by-pass your adversary, it will return you at once to the Swallows in the south. And for as long as the race survives you will be held up as an example to others – the bird who shamed his species, who to save his own skin betrayed his trust and allowed his beloved Princess to die.'

Swallow recalled the moment in the jungle, when he had been ready to accept that as his fate. He blushed with shame for then and now.

'Keep it safe. Use it wisely. And tell nobody,' Camel concluded.

Swallow promised and stowed the timer safely with his other treasures. Then Camel, smiling, said, 'Come on. Let's find Watt.'

He moved off back down the corridor and Swallow followed. Despite Camel's assurances that they would soon overtake Watt, it was some time and they were once more within sight of the orange trees before they at last caught up with him; and they only did so then because Watt stood stock-still, transfixed with horror at the sight that confronted him. They too looked; and they too were transfixed. A terrifying prospect lay before them.

One or two trees still stood, but the rest had gone and their place had been taken by a howling, swirling blackness. The Wild Wind and his troops, driven to madness by the goading dark, filled the chamber and obliterated it. They whistled, shrieked and roared – full of fury, but with no room to express it. They swirled round and round, crashed into each other and into the walls; engulfed the trees, shook them, made them sway and crack; but they were uanble, it seemed, to proceed past them until the last oranges had been extinguished. So they surged and foamed behind the trees, like a swollen sea, or turbulent waters about to burst through a dam.

Swallow was terrified; and Camel seemed to share his fear. It must be assumed that Watt did too, but nonetheless, once he had got over his initial shock, he still strove to continue on into the blackness to collect his precious helmet. Camel held him fast and told him the plan.

Watt protested that he couldn't let anyone else risk their lives for him. Camel, however, pointed out that while *his* life would certainly be in danger when he ventured into the chamber, Watt's – were he to do so – would undoubtedly be lost, and so would Swallow's and those of all his nation, perhaps those of all like-minded, light-loving creatures. Watt must decide, but he must think of others, and of other things besides his helmet.

Watt did think; and after much apparently deep thought, he agreed reluctantly to stay with Swallow. Camel nodded his approval. He then propped the branch up against the wall, told Swallow to remember his instructions and to perform them to the letter (this last very significantly – Swallow understood the significance and promised to remember), and then loped silently off up the corridor. He stopped by the first tree to select another branch, stood back and braced himself and looked behind him as though doubting the wisdom of his plan. His eyes seemed to glaze over again as he contemplated his private unspeakable horror and then they cleared, and he moved swiftly and silently between the trees and into the swirling blackness.

At once the swirling stopped. The blackness, taken by surprise, seemed to recoil slightly. Swallow and Watt held their breath. Silence. They prayed – Watt that he might be forgiven for letting Camel go in his stead, and Swallow that Camel might return safe and sound. And Camel that the light moving into their midst would confuse his enemies just long enough for him to get the helmet.

It did. With the orange branch still held out shield-like in front of him, he bent down, reached under the table, took the helmet in his mouth and started slowly, slowly back into the corridor.

This was the dangerous bit. So long as he advanced, the winds might be expected to retreat in confusion; but once he in turn retreated they would assume that he did so out of fear and then it was only a matter of time before they came back at him with redoubled venom. His hope was that he might reach the protection of the trees before they moved. And he nearly did. His hind legs, protruding between the trees, were already visible to Swallow and Watt when the winds struck.

Goaded from within the blackness, they overcame their fear of the lights and unleashed their fury on Camel. The protecting trees were sent crashing to the ground and their bright fruit was whisked up and away by whirlwinds who screamed with rage and with pain from where they scorched themselves. And Camel was picked up bodily, like Watt before him, and smashed into the wall on the far side of the corridor. His hind leg cracked against the wall. His head snapped back in a yelp of agony. The helmet flew from his mouth and rolled down the corridor.

Camel sank to the ground, but he held on to his orange branch. And now, dragging one leg uselessly behind him, he hobbled to the mouth of the corridor and stood there defiant, surrounded by furious, swirling blackness, but continuing by his presence to deny the dark wind access to the corridor and the friends.

Watt rushed up and grabbed his helmet. He rammed it firmly on his head and moved out to take his place alongside Camel. And Swallow reached into his pocket for the little bottle to restore him as it had formerly restored Watt.

But Camel, without looking round, said, 'No time. Go! Go! You must go!'

The blackness swirled around him. An orange fell from his branch and was at once whisked away into oblivion. Swallow and Watt hesitated.

'Go!' Camel commanded. 'I can't hold them for long. Go, or we'll all be lost!'

So they went. Watt picked up an orange to serve as a head-lamp, then leapt onto Swallow's back and they sped off down the corridor. As they turned the corner, Watt looked back and saw their champion – a lone defiant figure, a figure after his own heart – battered, cracked even, but unbowed, holding the winds at bay through sheer willpower. Another orange fell and vanished.

Swallow flew with new strength, born of the determination not to let Camel down, to be seen to be worthy of his sacrifice. He never paused for breath or stopped to look back. He heeded Camel's advice and followed his instinct. He went round bends, turned corners, crossed crossings and changed course several times with never a second thought. Second thoughts did indeed try to creep in every time, but always too late; and after a while they abandoned the attempt and his head was filled instead with a vision of the crippled Camel defying the swirling blackness at the mouth of the corridor, and of the oranges dropping one by one from his branch until it was bare. Then, with an ear-splitting explosion that shook the world, Swallow saw Camel smashed out of the way and the winds surge forward down the corridor.

Was it a vision? Or was it real? Was the Wind again playing tricks on him, making him see that which he feared? Using his imagination to show him what was really happening?

The corridor was shaking. Rocks crashed down all round them. Sand hung thick in the air.

It was real! Oh Lord, it was real! Camel really had been

destroyed! His eyes raining tears, Swallow flew yet faster. Oh Camel, poor Camel! Poor brave, heroic Camel! He heard the thunder of the winds behind, chasing them – faint at first, but growing louder by the second, rushing after them at such a pace that it seemed to Swallow that he was flying backwards.

The rumbling gained on them, till it was like an avalanche and they could hardly tell whether it came from behind or in front of them. Watt looked back and thought he saw something black and foaming, billowing after them down the corridor.

Swallow turned down a side corridor which ended in a heavy wooden door. He sprinted for it and landed by it, panting. He scarcely had the energy to reach into his pocket for the key. Watt turned the beam from his head-lamp back down the corridor. 'Quick. They'll be here.'

Swallow found the key and fumbled it into the lock. It seemed the wrong size. It wouldn't go in. And he had no strength, he couldn't force it. Had Camel made a mistake and given him the wrong key? Then it was in and he tried to turn it in vain.

Watt cried, 'Here they come!'

Swallow turned to see the swollen blackness surge around the corner.

'I can't open it,' he called.

'Let me have a go.' Watt gave Swallow the orange and grabbed the key. The blackness began to roll towards them.

Watt unlocked the door and swung it back on its hinges. 'Quick. Come on!' He took the orange from Swallow and pushed him through the doorway. Then he threw the orange at the approaching pitch, but it was at once swallowed up, as with a final rush the black mass poured roaring down the corridor.

Swallow was already pushing the door to. Watt, at the last moment, leapt back through the gap.

The swelling blackness was only yards away, an unstoppable tidal wave of evil. The door banged shut and at the same instant Swallow slid the bolt into place. Then he and Watt flattened themselves against the wall on either side of the door, expecting it at any moment to be smashed down and themselves, the door and everything else to be swept away into black oblivion.

Invisible in the blackness behind the door, the Prince's shadow smiled a silent smile. There were two reasons for his pleasure. The first was that the Wind had been cut down to size, which would save him a job. And the second, which he reflected on as he turned the key in the lock, was that the little adventurers now had no way back. They *had* to go on.

That being so, he saw no point in shadowing them further, but slipped off to spend his time more productively in making others suffer.

# 9

# Out of the Frying Pan . . .

It was some time before Swallow and Watt realised that the expected was not going to happen; and during that time they remained flattened and fearful against the wall on either side of the door – a pointless precaution had they thought about it, since if the winds were to smash the door down, no amount of flattening or cowering would save them. But practical efficacy has never been the main purpose of defensive postures against overwhelming enemies; and they felt better against the wall than they would have done standing out in front of the door. So there they stayed until they reassured themselves that the door was not going to come crashing in upon them.

Swallow's thoughts turned to Camel, to lament his passing.

And with these thoughts and as though prompted by them, there came memory of something Camel had said: 'First thoughts are your own; second thoughts may not be.'

'Yes,' said Swallow to himself, 'these are second thoughts, and they don't help. If Camel is dead – then he certainly didn't die for us to hang about feeling sorry for him, rather to get on as fast as we can.' He experienced a strange sense of approbation as he thought this, and knew that he was right. So he resolutely put his second thoughts behind him and turned his attention to what lay ahead.

He peered through the half-light, as Watt was already doing, and took in his surroundings. They were in what looked like a store room. A passageway stretched out in front of them, with shelving on either side. And on the shelving, packed tight one on top of the other, right up to the ceiling, were tins – large tubular tins, all the same size, all about twice the height of Swallow.

It *looked* like a storeroom, but it didn't feel like a store room – the atmosphere was heavy, charged and oppressive. It didn't sound like one – its silence was stifling. Nor did it smell like one – rather it stank of corruption and things rotten. Swallow winced and Watt held his nose. Both instinctively knew that smell – the stench of things going bad in confinement, the odour of putrefaction. It was the rancid reek of the dungeon.

And now for a moment and despite his resolution, second thoughts really did rush in on Swallow. They overwhelmed him. A dungeon! Had they raced out of the desert and into a dungeon? Had it all been an elaborate trap which they had flown into? He remembered in the jungle fleeing from the creepers and into the clutches of the Mamba. Had he now done it again? Had even Camel – he hardly dared think it – had even Camel been in on the deception, working for the Prince of Darkness, enmeshing them in a web of treachery, warning him against second thoughts, because those thoughts might reveal the truth – and his own duplicity?

Swallow felt as though the bottom had dropped out of his world. Nothing was certain any more. If Camel was an enemy, what of the secret life-timer that nestled in his pocket? What of Watt? He looked doubtfully across at him out of the corner of his eye and was at once reassured. Watt at least he could trust. But what good was that, if they were both of them all the time dancing to someone else's tune? If all their efforts, their successes as well as their failures, served someone else's purpose? Their enemy had known they were in the desert, had chased them all the way to the door, had, apparently, failed to catch them. But had he failed? Or had he, helped by Camel and the Wind, herded them into prison just as he wanted?

The doubts gnawed at Swallow's mind. He turned back to the door meaning to unbolt it and face whatever lay back there – blackness, Wind, whatever, rather than carry on with this crippling uncertainty. And, had he done so, second thoughts would have been joined by third, fourth and fifth ones, as his feeling of being toyed with seemed to be substantiated.

But he never unbolted the door. Before he could touch the bolt, Watt had diverted his attention away from the door and into the cell block. He too knew that this was a prison, but his reaction to the knowledge was very different from Swallow's – equally mistaken, but much more positive. His wayward little brain argued as follows:

'Prisons are for law-breakers. If there were no law-breakers, there would be no prisons. So the existence of prisons proves the existence of law-breakers, who've got to be restrained. And those who do the restraining are law-enforcement officers, like me, and to be assisted in any way possible.'

So, when an Ape complete with sword at his belt, big sea-boots, earring and eye-patch crossed the top of the corridor, Watt's inclination was to go over and greet him as a colleague. He started to move off. This it was which took Swallow's attention from the door. He flew after Watt down the passageway.

'Where d'you think you're going?'

'To see if he wants a hand.' Watt indicated where the Ape had just disappeared between the shelving.

'You don't think, do you?' said Swallow, not altogether fairly in the light of Watt's valiant but erring mental endeavour (nor in view of the less than helpful results of his own recent thinking). 'That is a Barbary Ape, a pirate, an outlaw, the enemy of all law and order.'

Watt's face blanched as Swallow completed the dictionary definition of a Barbary Ape: 'You mean – he's not a law-enforcement officer?'

'Not your law, he's not. He's in the service of the Prince of Darkness . . . and imprisoned in those tins will be creatures like us – all those who love the light – creatures like Rhino and Ox-pecker – those who might help us and be on our side.'

'And Camel?'

Swallow hesitated a moment, then conceded the point – Camel too was on their side. He wanted to believe it, so he would.

'Yes. Yes, and Camel.'

Watt seemed stunned by the revelation. He too hesitated, before commenting perceptively, 'You wouldn't get Camel in one of those tins. He's too big.'

'Well, not Camel necessarily, not Rhino necessarily – but creatures like them – our friends.'

'And anyway, if Camel was in there, it wouldn't have a picture like that on the front.'

'What?'

'The tins have all got pictures on them – orangey sort of pictures. See? Not Camel, are they?'

Swallow looked and sure enough, on the front of each tin, at about head height, there was a small square picture of a pair of smiling orange faces.

*Orange faces!* His mind flashed back to the start of his journey, to his meeting with More and Less. He recalled what they had told him: they hadn't heard from their cousins, the Tangerines, for some time and feared they must have been captured by the forces of darkness.

The Tangerines had been captured. The Apes were their captors. And this, unless Swallow was much mistaken, this was their prison.

He drew Watt back to the top of the corridor and put him in the picture. Watt was just about recovering from the earlier revelation. 'Oh,' he said, when Swallow had finished, 'oh dear. Nearly made a mess of that, didn't I?'

'You weren't to know. But we've got to help them. I promised More and Less I would. Judging by the smell, most of them must have died already, but some may still be alive and we can't just leave them.'

Watt agreed that that was out of the question and they set about thinking how they could help the prisoners out of their predicament. The first thing obviously was to get rid of the guards.

They stood still and listened. The Ape's footsteps echoed round the place, but there was no other sound. They could hear him walking up and down the corridors; he was coming nearer now, but out of sight. He must be walking towards them down a parallel passageway.

Swallow had an idea. He whispered to Watt, 'It sounds as if he's on his own. Look,' – he pointed up to the second level walkway – 'I'm going up there. I want you to stay here out of sight.' He steered Watt into the crevice between the first two tins at the top of the passageway. 'Don't move until I give the word. Then, when I do, get out as quick as you can into the middle of that cross-way, and stand there with your truncheon stretched out as far as it'll reach. Can you do that?'

''Course I can,' came the confident reply, 'easy as winkin'. But why?'

The footsteps were very close now. The Ape must be near the top of the corridor. Swallow cut the conversation short. 'Never mind, just do it. Keep out of sight until I say "Now", and then get out there as fast as you can.'

'With me truncheon out – yes. But what for? Is someone going to create a disturbance?' Watt gave one of his curious knee-bends.

'Perhaps.'

They heard the Ape turn the corner and start across towards them. Swallow left Watt and flew up to the second level, where he crouched down, his face towards the top of the corridor, trying not to breathe lest he give away their presence.

The footsteps approached, swaggering, self-confident.

Swallow braced himself. Down below he heard the crack of Watt's knuckles as he too got ready. The tiny sound rang round the cell block. Surely the Ape must have heard it. The foosteps seemed to stop. Silence.

Swallow feared that the Ape had been alerted and was even then creeping towards him. He expected a hairy hand to appear round the corner at any moment and grab him. The smell in the air seemed to grow heavier, ranker, to mingle with the smell of his own fear.

Then the footsteps started again. One, two, one, two, ever closer, just round the corner. One, two. One more and then . . .

The Ape's profile appeared at the top of the corridor.

Swallow gave the word 'Now', and flew with all his might straight at him, targetting on the one visible ear.

The Ape turned to face him. 'What the dev –' He looked straight at the feathered bullet. His hand came up to protect his face, and his whole body jerked back. In doing so his big sea-boot tripped over Watt's outstretched truncheon. He toppled headlong backwards into the wall.

His head smashed against it with a crack like that of a whip. He gave one painful gasp and his body sagged to the floor. He rolled over and was still.

Swallow would have felt proud at the success of his plan, but before he had time to feel anything, two more Apes, alerted by the noise, had rushed out of a small doorway at the far end of the corridor.

'What's going on? Trouble is it?'

They peered into the darkness and were just able to make out the form of their comrade lying face downwards at the top of the corridor, his cutlass still in his belt, pointing up in the air towards them.

'Looks like they got Alonso.'

'What – a break-out is it?'

They drew their swords and tore along the passageway.

'Yer yeller-bellied little glow worms. Come out whur we c'n see yer!'

'Come out, yer little glimmers! Come out 'ere and we'll put yurr light out f'r good 'n' all.'

Taken by surprise, it was all Swallow could do to fly up to the topmost walkway out of their reach. But evasive action never entered Watt's head. Swallow's ploy for knocking out Alonso had taught him a new trick and he hastened down the corridor to see if it would work again.

The Apes kept coming, cutlasses swinging, searching the cell-block for some foe worthy of the name. The first one neared the top of the corridor. Watt stood there, truncheon out, braced for contact. The Ape reached the top and peered round the corner. His foot caught on Watt's truncheon. He lost his balance and toppled towards the prone Alonso. Alonso's cutlass pierced him like a skewer. He gave a gasp and hung there.

His colleague behind saw it all, as if in slow motion, but was himself moving too fast to avoid the pile-up. He tripped over his colleague's boots, fell forward and impaled himself on the protruding point of the cutlass. He too breathed his last and the three of them hung there, skewered on the cutlass, like some monstrous Ape-kebab.

Watt returned his truncheon to its pocket in his trouser leg and thought with grim satisfaction that, if there were justice in the world, all pirates would end up like this. Swallow shuddered at the sight and felt a little sick. He shrank from the thought that he had caused this carnage.

But there was time neither for remorse nor self-satisfaction. There might be yet more Apes in the room at the end of the corridor, and even if there were not, the noise might attract others from outside. If they were to release the Tangerines, they must move quickly.

Swallow whispered to Watt, 'Come on, let's see if there are any more.'

Silently they slipped along the corridor and came to a halt beside the doorway. They listened for any sound which might indicate the presence of another pirate. But there was none.

Slowly, cautiously, Watt peered round the foot of the doorway. The room was empty. They went in.

This was clearly the guardroom. The furniture was a bare wooden table, flanked by benches. On the table steamed three large mugs of grog – two half-empty and one (obviously Alonso's) still full.

The walls were lined with cutlasses, all glistening deadly sharp; grappling hooks and marline spikes; thumbscrews, chains and manacles, – all the usual paraphernalia of a pirate prison.

But none of this interested Swallow and Watt. What they were looking for were the keys to the cells. A bunch of keys lay beside one of the mugs on the table. Swallow picked it up and – with some difficulty, for they were large keys by his standards – flew back up the corridor. But when he examined the tins he discovered that none of them had key-holes. The keys were useless.

Again Swallow felt the second thoughts coming at him, counselling despair; but he couldn't listen to them now – friends' lives were at stake, he couldn't let them down. He forced himself to go on. There was a way to open the tins. There must be. He had to find it.

He felt down the seams of the tins for some secret button or catch that would open them. He tried one. He tried another and another. But it was no good.

Watt stopped him. 'They must have been sealed in. So they'll have to be cut out.'

'How?'

'A tin opener?'

A tin opener! Of course. Swallow was annoyed that he hadn't thought of it himself; 'I didn't see any in the guardroom. Did you?'

'No. I expect they carry them with them.'

They went back to the skewered Apes at the top of the corridor; and, once there, Watt dived fearlessly into the midst of the blood-soaked stack, vanished for a second, then reappeared wiping his hands and crying: 'Here we are!'

He was pointing to a fearsome-looking tin opener, which

hung from Alonso's belt. It comprised a long handle, which enfolded a deadly corkscrew blade, and at the top a razor-sharp, pointed tin opener, and a bludgeoning, head-cracking bottle opener. It was about as tall as Swallow was long.

Watt quickly undid Alonso's belt and then the two of them removed the tin opener and slipped across to the cells.

The next step was to find a cell which was still occupied by a live Tangerine. They walked along the row, tapping on the front of the tins and calling, 'Who's in there?' From the first five they got no response, but their knock on the sixth produced the very faintest of answers. So faint that they doubted they had heard it. They knocked again: 'Who's in there?'

'812517 prisoner Tangerine T.'

'836105 prisoner Tangerine S for Sugar.'

'We're friends,' Swallow called back. 'Stand clear. We're going to open the tin.' And without more ado they laid into the front of the tin with the sharp point of the tin opener. It pierced through the cell wall as a knife slices butter, and in no time at all the front of the tin was unzipped, the door rolled back, and the imprisoned Tangerines scrambled out.

Remembering the Orangelands, Swallow had expected the prison to be instantly lit up when the Tangerines were released. He thought of each cell as a bubble of light trapped in a sea of darkness. But he was disappointed: there was no lightening of the gloom when these poor, shrivelled, stinking specimens staggered out. If anything, their misery made the gloom even heavier. They were like coals spat from a fire: no doubt they retained some heat at their core, but the light had quite left their faces.

They stood there and shivered: 'Who are you? Where do you come from? It's not a trick is it? Not another trick – please don't play any more tricks on us.'

'No,' said Swallow, 'it's not a trick. We were sent by your cousins, the Orangemen.'

At the mention of their cousins, and even more at the sight of the orange seeds, which Swallow produced as proof of his good faith, the Tangerines took courage and expressed their readiness to do whatever was required.

Watt had already moved further along the cell row, tapping, calling, listening for any answer.

Swallow told the Tangerines to take time to recover, to let their eyes get used to the light. And then to help to release their friends. He thought they might find more tin openers in the belts of the two other skewered pirates. Then he went over to join Watt.

The Tangerines swelled almost visibly. Their eyes focussed; their muscles hardened. They were still scrawny, but no longer limp. They moved purposefully over to the pirates and commandeered their openers.

By the time Swallow rejoined Watt he had found another occupied cell and together they peeled back the front and released the occupants. On the far side of the passageway, the Tangerines did the same.

More and more Tangerines were released. They poured out of their cells, took a moment to grasp the situation, then pulled themselves together and set to. The room rang with the sound of tin opener on tin, and released Tangerines soon filled the floor and walkways, demanding to know what was to be done next and insisting that, whatever it was, Swallow and Watt should lead them.

'We can't. We haven't time,' Swallow shouted up to them. 'We've got to get to England to fight the Prince of Darkness. He's been following us, and always up to now he's made us do what he wants. This is the first time we've done something he wasn't ready for. So we must get on before he can turn it to his advantage.'

Still the Tangerines pleaded for leadership.

'No,' said Swallow, 'we've released you. Now it's up to you.' He turned to Watt: 'Come on. Let's see if we can find a way out.' But Watt didn't move. 'Come on!'

'No.'

'What?'

'No. I can't just fly off and leave the Apes behind undefeated. You can maybe. But I can't.'

Swallow felt the anger rising inside him. For heaven's sake

– didn't they have enough problems, without Watt being difficult? 'Look – we've released the Tangerines. Now they must fight their own battles. We've got to get away. Come on.'

'No. It's not just their battle. It's mine too. You go.'

Watt was immovable. Swallow saw it, stifled his anger and bowed to the inevitable: 'All right, all right. But we can't stay for long.'

'Hooray!' chorused the Tangerines. 'Hooray! Tell us what to do.'

They all looked expectantly at Swallow. Swallow looked expectantly at Watt. And Watt blushed and wondered what was expected of him.

'Well, come on,' said Swallow, allowing his irritation to show, 'tell us what to do.'

'Well, we'll . . . fight them, of course . . .' Watt ventured at last. 'We'll go out and fight them . . .'

'We can't,' said Swallow, 'not if we want to win. They're too big, too fierce, and there are far too many of them. Suggest something else.'

Watt tried. He gave all the appearance of deep thought: his brow furrowed; his eyes narrowed; his arms crossed and the fingers of one hand beat an irregular tattoo on his upper lip. But the appearance was deceptive: Watt's mind remained a perfect blank. He knew what he must do: fight the Apes. Something deep inside told him that. But how? That was another matter.

'I can't think of anything,' he said. 'I can't.'

All eyes turned to Swallow. Reluctantly he accepted the responsibility, and thought. He too found it hard. Up to now his enemies had always sought him out, ambushed him, and he'd only had to defend himself. This was the first time he'd had to plan an attack. He thought of all he'd ever heard about Apes. They were cruel, vicious, lawless – great fighters. They were noisy and respected noise in others. They had a reputation for being great cowards if they were ever outnumbered, but as they usually outnumbered their opponents by four or five to one, that was hard to prove.

Hard to prove perhaps, but worth a try. Swallow looked at

the eager, waiting Tangerines and at the rows of cells behind them. He had an idea.

'You can't fight the Apes,' he said, 'but it's just possible that you may be able to frighten them. Here's what I suggest . . .'

The Tangerines listened agog. Watt too.

'Stay here. Let your comrades out. Then cut up thc tins and make yourselves instruments – drums, cymbals, whatever you can. When you've done that, wait. Watt and I will go out and try to create a diversion. If we succeed, I'll give you two sharp tweets, like this –' He demonstrated a high-pitched call, not loud in volume, but very piercing. 'Right?'

They nodded.

'When you hear that, start banging your instruments as loud and as hard as you can. Do it for about half a minute, then come out – still banging. If the noise is loud enough and seems to be coming for them, it might just frighten the Apes off.'

He paused, awaiting a reaction. Then he added apologetically. 'Anyway, it's all I can suggest. What do you say?'

Silence. Then:

'Yes,' said Watt.

'Yes,' echoed the Tangerines, as one.

'Right,' said Swallow, 'get on with it.'

The Tangerines needed no second invitation. They set to at once opening tins, ripping off doors, assembling and tuning up the percussion. Swallow and Watt quickly cut fragments off the Apes' clothing and improvised pirate garb for themselves, so that, though tiny, they would not otherwise look out of place among the Apes. Their only problem was with Watt's helmet, which of course he insisted on wearing and which, despite being swathed in a piece of Ape's bandana, still looked far from convincing as pirate head-gear. But it would have to do, they had no time for improvements. They must move quickly, or the Apes would come to prevent them.

He took Watt on his back and they flew over the industrious Tangerines to the far end of the cell block. There they unlocked the barred door with the keys they had found on the guard-room table, swung the door open and slipped out into the Apes' stronghold.

# 10

# . . . And Into an Argument

A spiral staircase carved out of the rock wound away from them. Slowly, warily, they started to climb. They expected the unexpected at any moment, were ready for any eventuality. They had to be. For, as Swallow had pointed out, these Apes were outlaws: they didn't abide by rules. There was no knowing when or where they would strike; and if you hoped for a fair fight you hoped in vain, for from an Ape's point of view there was no fun fighting if you had to be fair. No, with Barbary Apes the only rule was that there were no rules and that you had to be always on your guard. So Swallow and Watt crept cautiously up the staircase, a step at a time and pausing frequently to listen for the excited jabbering of the Ape who thinks he's on to a good thing.

The hammering and banging died away behind them and they carried on in silence. Swallow imagined silent Apes everywhere; smiling, waiting. He longed for some sound to be frightened of, a focus for his fear.

From somewhere above them a small sound pricked the silence. They stopped and listened. Nothing. They must have imagined it. They went on. No – there it was again, carried to them on the breeze, distinctly now: a bustling sound. As they listened it filled out, took shape: feet were scurrying, whistles blowing, heavy weights being banged down. And every so often there was a sharp crack that seemed to hang in the air and to make the feet above move even faster. And underneath it all and so unexpected that Swallow scarcely believed his ears, the familiar sound of water lapping and ships' timbers creaking. Water? In the middle of the Atlas Mountains? Surely not.

They listened again and there could be no mistake: what they heard was the sound of a boat riding at anchor. They inched their way up the staircase. Daylight began to reach them, thin and grey, as though it had been strained through storm clouds: the dregs of daylight. Another of the strange sharp cracks rang out. Feet ran. Ape voices jabbered. Seagulls squawked. Soon they saw the Gulls wheeling across the lowering grey sky. Then they were up, level with the top and Swallow was able to complete the picture.

They had come out on to a quayside, where a great galleon lay at anchor. Apes swarmed all over it, making it ready for some voyage. They scurried up and down the gang plank; they swung busily in the rigging; they showered sparks sharpening cutlasses; they spliced ropes and primed cannon; and all with such urgency as though the next moment might be their last.

The quay ran along the side of an inlet leading out to the open sea. It was sheltered on either side by massive cliffs, sheer rock-faces – dull grey freckled with black dots – which beetled thousands of feet above their heads.

So this was the Apes' stronghold, the hide-out to which they returned whenever the forces of the law threatened. No wonder they'd always been able to escape their pursuers. It was the perfect retreat: inaccessible from the land; invisible and impregnable from the sea.

Swallow gazed in awe at the magnificence of it. And in doing so he became aware of an intricate pattern of movement, ant-like across the cliff-face, from freckle to freckle. He looked more closely and his awe changed into horror. Ants had almost been right. The freckles were caves. The cliffs were honeycombed with caves like giant ant-hills. Only in this case the Ants were Apes.

Watt drew his attention back to the quayside and to two figures farther along who stood out from the rest. Their appearance and bearing suggested Apes in authority. The first one stood out for the most obvious of reasons: he was four times the size of any other, sported an enormous black beard, and held in his hand a great whip, which he cracked with relish at the heels of any Ape who came within reach.

*Crack!* An Ape jumped, squealing. Others ran.

Swallow realised that this was the strange, unidentified sound they had heard – the crack of the whip echoing round the hidden recesses of the pirates' nest. And he was left in no doubt as to the kind of creature he had to deal with, for with his next crack the great Ape calmly sliced one of his underlings neatly down the middle – for no other reason apparently than that he was handy, and it was better to practise on the real thing, then to waste one's efforts on empty air. The two halves of the hapless pirate teetered on the quayside for a moment as if trying to stick themselves together, then toppled over into the water. The Ape, concerned about his technique, repeated the stroke, carving the air where the body had been. Then he looked round for another victim. No wonder the feet scurried when the whip rang out.

The only one unaffected by all this was the great Ape's companion – a diminutive figure, as small as the other was large. In fact he didn't look like an Ape at all. A Monkey, yes, of some sort. But not an Ape.

He had the enormous saucer-shaped eyes that Swallow associated with the night Monkeys – the Lorises and Lemurs. He was clean-shaven; and in contrast to the others who were dressed in traditional pirate clothes, he wore a blue-velvet tail coat and white satin breeches, both of which fitted perfectly and suggested that he had an excellent tailor. On his head he wore a three-cornered hat edged with gold braid. And in his right hand he held a delicate lace handkerchief. This he dabbed constantly at his nostrils, and seemed by this means to shut out all the unpleasantness that surrounded him – including the obtrusive death of the publicity-seeking pirate.

The two were approaching along the quayside, deep in conversation. Swallow and Watt drew back down the stairs out of sight.

The big one was talking: 'I an't frighted o' no Orangemen. But I don' see no point sailin' all th' way down thur, when thur's plenty o' pickin's yur.'

'The point, my dear, brainless Blackbeard,' the little one replied, 'the point is that they have defied our master, the Prince of Darkness. And our master, Blackbeard, does not like to be defied.' He spoke quietly, but his words carried a threat.

Blackbeard did not miss the point: ''Course. I knows that . . .'

'Good. Then you will have the boat loaded and be off on the evening tide. You like smashing things; and the Orangemen are to be smashed. So off you go and have fun.'

'Fun!' grumbled Blackbeard. 'Th' only fun I warnts is t'be lef' 'lone t' get on wi' my piratin'. Blarsted nuisance! Why can' 'e let 'em be?'

He finished with another vicious crack of the whip, which all but decapitated Watt, whose curiosity had drawn him forward and who now backed sharply off again. But neither of them noticed and the little one (Swallow was now convinced that he was a Lemur) repeated himself with some impatience: 'Because they have defied him. They have shed light where there should be darkness. They have passed their secrets on to a Swallow; and he and his companion, a puerile policeman, have entered the realms of darkness and challenged the Prince's power.'

(Watt's hackles rose: 'Is that me he's talking about?')

'They blinded the Master and the Wild Wind with a ghastly orange light! Orange light, Blackbeard! In the dark of the desert! Can you imagine?'

('I'm not puerile!')

'It made our Master angry. It made him very angry indeed. And the offenders are to suffer.'

('I'm not – am I?'

'Of course not. Ssssh.')

'The Swallow will be dealt with in due course. But the Orangemen are to be punished at once and by you.'

Still Blackbeard was doubtful: 'Orange light? In th' desert? Sounds like desert lightnin' t' me. 'Ow do 'e know they brought it with 'em?'

'Because he shadowed them, of course. How do you think? He shadowed them as he shadows all his enemies. Just as he'll shadow you, if you don't do as you're told.'

'All right, all right. We'll go. But what 'appens aft'r? When th' Orangemen's conqu'red 'n' ev'rywhur's dark? What d'we do then?'

'Then?' laughed the Lemur. 'Why, then we shall see.'

And they moved along the quayside out of earshot.

Again there were the old familiar thoughts hammering at Swallow's temples, clamouring for admission, eager to get in and argue the case for despair. But he kept them out. This was not the time. There would be a time for thoughts, even for despair; but this was not it. The Lemur had told him nothing new – it was just that it seemed new hearing someone else saying it. He had long suspected that he had been followed and that his every move was known to his adversary. But was that a reason for him to stand by while More and Less and their fellows suffered on his account? Could he allow that to happen? Well – could he?

His resolution was stiffened by Watt who still smarted under the label of 'puerile' (whatever it might mean) and was determined that the Lemur should be made to eat his words. Policemen are *never* puerile! (Or, if they ever are, are certainly not to be called so.)

They put their heads together and considered ways in which the Apes might be stopped. Frightening them off with noise and superior numbers now seemed to be out of the question, for not only were the Apes big and undeniably fierce, but they easily outnumbered the Tangerines as well.

Watt suggested that Swallow have a word with the Seagulls – after all, there were enough of them, and an aerial strike might prove very effective. But, as Swallow explained, Gulls were not to be trusted. They were themselves pretty lawless, and would be just as likely to deliver Swallow and Watt over to the Apes, as to help them prevent the pirates' voyage.

No, if the Apes were to be stopped, they must somehow be made to stop themselves. Swallow's mind went back to the conversation between Blackbeard and the Lemur. The tensions were there, if only they could exploit them. They had been arguing: the Lemur had said that the Orangemen were to be 'smashed'. 'You like smashing things,' he had said. 'So off you go and have fun.' But Blackbeard had not found the prospect very amusing: 'What 'appens aft'r?' he had asked. 'When th' Orangemen's conqu'red 'n' ev'rywhur's dark?' 'Then?' the Lemur had laughed into his handkerchief. 'Why, then we shall see.'

'What happens when the Orangemen are conquered and everywhere is dark?'

Well – what would happen? The Prince of Darkness would rule, and everyone would obey. Everyone – including the Apes. But – just a minute – the Apes were outlaws, pirates, they lived in defiance of authority. How could they obey? Of course, that was it, that was what Blackbeard was worried about. So long as authority was on the side of good, evil and lawlessness went hand in hand. But what happened when darkness was enthroned everywhere? What happened to pirates then? As Blackbeard suspected, they would have to become law-abiding citizens. The Barbary Apes would be no more. Piracy would be a thing of the past. That was why Blackbeard was so unwilling to sail against the Orangemen: not because he liked them, or disliked the thought of hurting them, but because he saw that their defeat would bring that much closer the day of universal dark.

That was the fear the Swallow must exploit. He must foment this argument and make it erupt into war – the forces of evil against those of lawlessness – get them to destroy each other, then whistle up the Tangerines to pick up the pieces.

His mind raced. It was no good for either he or Watt to try and talk to them: they would probably not be heard, or, if they were, would certainly be ignored. No, the warning must come from some power, some oracle that the Apes respected. Some oracle? Swallow gazed abstractedly at the honey-combed cliff-face. The Spirit of the Mountains, perhaps? No. The Voices of Apes Past? Nearer, but no. The . . . the . . . Swallow smiled . . . The Great Ape of Atlas! That was it: the Great Ape of Atlas – the mythical ancestor of these Apes, reputed to be buried at the end of the longest tunnel, at the bottom of the deepest cavern, the guardian spirit to whom the Apes prayed before every voyage. If he could be made to appear, he would certainly have the necessary authority. Swallow beckoned Watt closer and whispered in his ear. Watt listened with growing amazement, then said incredulously, 'What, me?'

'Who else?'

'They'll never swallow it.'

'Yes, they will.' Swallow pointed up to the caves. 'Go up there. Find the largest cave you can. Make sure no-one's around. Then go in and start speaking. And be quick: you heard what he said – they're sailing on the evening tide.'

Watt was off like a whippet. He pulled the bandana down over his helmet and was gone, along the quayside and up the rocks. Swallow watched him go, but so good was Watt's imitation of the arrogant Ape swagger, that it was not long before he lost him in the crowd.

There was nothing now for Swallow to do but wait; and waiting, at last and inevitably, to admit the thoughts. He sat back and expected that, as before, they would come crowding in upon him. No thought made the attempt. It seemed that now that he was ready for them, they were no longer interested. He tried to lure them in by casting his mind back to that first moment in the dungeon, when he'd realised that they'd flown out of the desert and into prison, when he had mentally coupled Camel and the Prince of Darkness together as accomplices in the great deception. The thoughts now refused to make the connection, and Camel's name (much to Swallow's relief) was cleared. He recalled the words of the Lemur – that the Prince of Darkness had shadowed them all the way, and that he was to be dealt with in due course. The recollection no longer prompted panic or despair, rather a stoical acceptance that if that was his fate, then so be it.

Only he did wonder (and not for the first time) at the silliness of it all: the silliness of him seeking such a fate, setting out to take on the Prince of Darkness. It was all so disproportionate – no wonder the Councillors had laughed. Heavens above, but for a large dose of luck, any one of the enemies he had met so far (and they were as nothing to the one still to come) could have finished him off ten times over! Silly bird, he thought.

He pictured all the places he would rather be – places he had been and could still be, had he chosen sensibly: Rhino's garden; the Orangelands (he might still have been playing that game of 'Hunt the Orange'); his barn in the south. His barn. Oh, it would be good to be back there. If he could somehow be transported back there, you wouldn't find him leaving again in a hurry. No, not even to get to England.

From wistfully wishing, a small almost imperceptible sideways leap found him thinking: couldn't he? Couldn't he transport himself back there? Of course he could – at any moment he chose. He had the means in his pocket. All he had to do was to decide to use it.

He reached into his pocket and brought out the timer. Camel had said that if he turned it upside down before its due time, it would return him to the Swallows in the south. True, he had added that if he did so to shorten his journey or to avoid his enemy, then his return would be a shameful one. But he had said nothing about a case like this, where Swallow simply decided that he was not the bird for the job, that he had made a mistake. In such a case, he felt sure, if he turned the timer upside down, he would at once find himself back in his barn, no questions asked, no blame attached. All he had to do was turn the timer. He stared at it, wondering. Would he? Could he?

He leant his head back against the wall and closed his eyes. Confused images flashed through his brain: Watt triumphant in the fork of the mahogany tree, his flying towards him meaning to save him, but instead blowing him off his perch and into the cliff face, battering him relentlessly against the rock. Watt looking, imploring, becoming Camel. Still smashing. Hearing the sickening crack as his leg broke. Camel looking, imploring, collapsing to the foot of the cliff and changing again – to Princess Hiro lying on her cold dark death-bed. He no longer blowing; standing beside her. She looking, imploring, speaking: 'Don't let me die, Swallow.'

Swallow opened his eyes, looked at the timer, and answered his own question. No. No, he wouldn't turn it – he couldn't. Even though he had chosen to come on this perilous journey, he could not now choose to return. He was no longer a free agent: friendship, suffering, love, all created obligations.

He put the timer back in his pocket. He had to go on.

Inside his head Princess Hiro still begged, 'Don't let me die. I want to see the Sun shine again over England. Help me, Swallow. Help me...' And inside his head Swallow answered, 'You shall see England, Princess. You shall dance again in the summer sunshine. I shall watch you swoop over rippling rivers and across fields full of buttercup and daisy to the humming of the Bee and the lowing of the Cow. And we shall sit in the eaves and I shall love you, Princess.'

'Promise me, Swallow. Promise me.'

And quietly Swallow promised. Silently he swore that no matter how far or how long he must go on, no matter how hopeless the odds against him were, nor what horrors his enemies had prepared for him – he would never give up or go back. No, never again think back, until either he or the forces of darkness were destroyed. And so, although he didn't realise it at the time, Swallow faced the thoughts (whose subtlety it was never to appear in the form expected of them) and put them once and for all behind him.

Even as he did so, a great booming voice rang out above his head. He ducked instinctively, expecting at any moment to be grabbed by an enormous hand, or split in two by the lash of the whip. But the voice continued to boom and neither hand nor whip sought him out.

On the quayside the footsteps stopped; the jabbering for once was stilled. Everyone listened: *Beware, Blackbeard! Beware! Beware!*

The words came again and again: *Beware!*

*The Dark One will use you to smash all his foes.*
*Beware! For he's leading the Apes by the nose.*
*By killing them off, you destroy yourselves too*
*And that's just what the Dark One intends you to do.*
*Beware Blackbeard! Beware the day,*
*When the Barbary Apes will be made to obey... obey...*
*obey...*

The voice faded away, to be succeeded by silence; then a disgruntled muttering. Swallow smiled – Watt was wonderful: the idea of speaking in rhyme was a touch of genius – just the way oracles spoke. And the message was getting home. The Apes were divided; some still favoured smashing the Orangemen and cared nothing for the consequences; but others were worried by the warning – they'd never been accused of being obedient before. Tempers rose. 'Who are you?' shouted Blackbeard, his voice sounding very feeble by comparison.

*The Great Ape of Altas,* came the booming reply.

The Apes gasped. The voice continued:

*Consider, Blackbeard, that when Darkness rules,*
*The Apes will be known as the Prince's fools... fools...*
*fools...*

The word was still echoing round the inlet, when the Lemur's shrill treble cut in, high-pitched and frantic.

'Don't listen to him! It's a trick. Someone's trying to set us against each other.'

But Blackbeard was worried: 'What does 'appen to us, when 'e rules?'

'I told you. There will be a place for you.'

'What kind o' place?'

'I don't know – a place. What does it matter? You swore allegiance. You promised...'

'On condition.'

'You promised to serve the Prince.'

'And 'e promised to protect us 'n' our way o' life.' The debate was taking place over an angry hum of discontented jabberings. Blackbeard had to shout to make himself heard: ''Ow do I know 'e'll keep 'is promise?'

'He's the Prince of Darkness. He always keeps his promise.'

'And I's Cap'n o' th' Apes. I always breaks mine!' came Blackbeard's final and unanswerable retort.

It was the signal the Apes had been waiting for. With cutlasses drawn, clubs swinging, hands, feet and hair flying, they laid into one another. Some cried 'Up evil! Long live the Lemur!', while others proclaimed themselves followers of 'Blackbeard the Bold'. But in reality they didn't seem to mind much whether they fought friend or foe, so long as they fought. All thought of the ship, the trip to the south, or of anything other than carving pieces out of each other, was banished from their minds. Limbs flew like skittles; heads rolled along the quayside like bowls; and enough eyes were knocked out to furnish a good game of marbles. With all the hurly-burly no-one heard the two tweets that Swallow gave to summon up the Tangerines.

But they heard what happened next. From deep within the hillside came an angry rumbling. The fighting stopped. The Apes listened, wary. The rumbling continued. The cliffs seemed to shake. The Gulls flew squawking into the air. On the quayside there was not a sound. The rumbling grew louder, fiercer. Swallow heard a whisper: 'The Ape of Atlas is angry.'

Other voices took it up. The rumbling was coming closer. The noise chased round the recesses of the pirates' nest, back and forth across the inlet. It grew angrier by the minute. It was like an earthquake, or a volcano about to erupt. Apes, who a moment before had been at each other's throats, clung together for comfort.

'The Ape of Atlas is angry!'

A bright shaft of light shot up into the sky, its beams slicing through the grey. Rumbling and light approached, growing all the time.

'See where 'e comes. We've offended 'im!'

Still it approached. It was almost upon them. The noise, bouncing back and forth, was enormous. The world seemed about to burst. The bright beam, like the eye of an avenging god, searched out the Apes. They panicked.

''E's comin' t' destroy us! 'E's comin' t' destroy us! Quick!'

With Blackbeard at their head they jumped, dived and tumbled into the water. Some were drowned; others pushed under or trodden on; a few escaped out to sea. All disappeared. The Lemur did so too. Seeing the way things were going, he scampered off up the cliff and vanished down the deepest of the caves. Swallow covered his ears, closed his eyes and cowered in his corner. The ear-splitting, blinding torrent sweep over him and erupted onto the quayside.

Swallow felt a tap on his shoulder. He opened his eyes and looked round. An exultant Watt grinned down at him: 'Worked a treat, didn't it?'

'Did it?'

''Course.'

'I thought the hillside was erupting.'

'So did the Apes. I've never seen anyone move so fast.'

'But if the hill didn't... then what was all that...?' Swallow never finished the question. He gazed up. The once drab sky was bathed in orange light.

'Come up and see.'

He climbed out onto the quayside. A great cheer went up. He stood there, blinking blindly. When he stopped he saw that he was surrounded by Tangerines. They held their improvised instruments in their hands and cheered to the echo. It seemed they were cheering him but Swallow failed to see why. They must have taken advantage of the eruption and come out in its wake. He was glad. But still he saw no source for all the light. He looked round, half expecting to see the Great Ape of Atlas beaming down at him. He turned to Watt, who grinned from ear to ear as though enjoying some huge private joke.

'Where's all the light coming from?' Swallow asked.

Watt didn't answer, but called out, '812517 prisoner Tangerine T. 836105 prisoner Tangerine S for Sugar, one pace forward. March!'

Two Tangerines stepped smartly forward, bright, glowing, grinning at Swallow. Swallow blinked again. His mind flicked back to the moment in the cell block, when they had peeled back the door and these two had staggered out, shivering, stinking, colourless. The truth dawned. Swallow grinned. He giggled. And before he knew what was happening, they were all laughing uncontrollably. The Tangerines had got back their colour! They were glowing again! That was why the quayside was lit up, why the clouds were pushed back. The Tangerines had revived. Theirs was the rumbling; theirs the savage, searching beam of light; and theirs now the laughter that chased the sombre echoes out of the pirates' nest. Swallow felt the first stirrings of real hope.

He turned to Watt: 'Now – are you ready to go on?'

Watt, still laughing, said, 'Yes. Yes, now I'm ready.'

'Well, come on then.'

They removed their pirate gear and tossed it into the water. Watt climbed aboard, they said farewell to the Tangerines and flew up and away.

'Goodbye! Thank you! Thank you!' chorused the Tangerines, beaming up at them.

'Well,' said Watt, 'that's one place the light's not quite gone out.'

'Yes,' agreed Swallow. 'And it won't be the only one.'

# 11

# The Vale of Tears

They pierced through the orange ceiling and plunged, like divers into muddy water, into greyness: greyness everywhere – on the ground and in the sky. It was hard to tell where one stopped and the other began. And the further they flew, the more the greyness seeped into everything and seemed to rot it to the core.

The earth had sickened. It lay under its blanket of cloud like an invalid, cold and shivering. Life had become a joyless struggle for survival. Creatures moved in pain: they would sooner have stood still, but something forced them forward. Birds fought grimly against the air currents as though they had forgotten how to fly, but dared not admit it. Bushes and trees huddled close to the ground, striving to be invisible; and flowers, once bright beacons which sent signals flashing out across the meadows, were now ashen embers flickering fitfully, calling to no-one.

Swallow recalled the France of fable – the cross-roads of Europe, where migrants heading north, east and west met and mingled before travelling on to their summer homes; a land of hope, a land of promise. And he wondered what hope this sickly land held out to him. What promise could this grey, rotting country possibly make? He knew the answer; and he rejected it. But not before a little of the greyness had seeped into him.

The flight was hard going. Where before he had reached speeds of fifty or more miles an hour, now it was all he could do to make fifteen; and the effort it cost him was enormous. The countryside below was so forbidding that he would gladly have flown over it without stopping; but at this speed that was no longer possible – it would take days. Besides, beyond France lay the North Sea and, presumably, the Prince of Darkness; and how could they hope to face him, let alone outwit him, if they arrived exhausted from days of non-stop travelling? No: they must stop and rest.

They looked round for the least forbidding spot. For a long time everywhere looked equally inhospitable, but at last Watt pointed over to his right, to a broad bottomed valley, surrounded by thickly-wooded hillsides. It was completely cut off from the outside world and so promised a minimum of disturbance. Large numbers of birds busied themselves in the fields. Obviously in better times this must have been prime pasture and a favourite haunt of local birds; but now, though the denseness of the woods gave the trees a little more self-confidence, and the birds in the fields seemed free to move about as they chose, even so, the depth of misery that came up at them as they descended, was such that it took their breath away.

They landed towards the western side of a large meadow. Of the birds already there, not one looked up to take note of their arrival.

Swallow thought how sick of life the poor creatures must be: he could have been a Cat or a Fox, a Snake, a Stoat, any predator coming to catch and kill them, yet they made no effort to escape. Each bird seemed to be saying 'Here I am – take me!'

And now that he saw them more closely, Swallow could understand why. The birds were wrecks: nothing but skin, bone and a scant supply of ragged, dirty feathers. And what made it all the more distressing was that they were wrecks of fine, beautiful birds. Closest to them was what had once been a Hoopoe. But where its crest had been it was now quite bald, and the bold barring on its wings was marred by missing feathers. As it picked at the dank grass it sobbed 'Hoo-hoo-hoo' a sad echo of its once-proud call. Beyond it, a Golden Oriole silently tried to bury its head in a tussock of grass. Swallow's heart went out to it. The few yellow feathers it had left were smudged with dirt, and elsewhere its grey skin lay bare for all to see and for the wet and the wind to pierce.

Swallow turned his head away: such things shouldn't be looked at. But everywhere it was the same. Birds decayed on every side. Here a pair of Turtle Doves huddled together – their pink breasts featherless and pinched, each ashamed to find itself still loved by the other. There a Heron stumbled over the ground, long neck drooping, tears pouring from eyes which saw nothing but the reflection of their own misery. And many more all in the same condition: a Ruff, a pair of Shovellers, a Curlew or two, more Hoopoes. All kinds of birds from all kinds of habitats; but Swallow saw at once that they had one thing in common with each other and with himself: they were all migrants. But in that case, they couldn't have been here for very long, since migrants all travel at much the same season. Had their decay then been so quick? Why? What had caused it? Did the same fate attend him? Was this some horror even he had not foreseen?

Very gently, so as not to frighten him, they approached the nearest Hoopoe.

'Hello. I'm Swallow.'

'And I'm Watt.'

'Hoo-hoo-hoo,' sobbed the Hoopoe.

'What's the matter?' asked Swallow. 'Why are you all so wretched?'

'Hoo-hoo,' repeated the Hoopoe.

With the sure instinct of the born interrogator, Watt came straight to the point: 'It's that blessed Prince of Darkness, isn't it?'

'Hoo hoo.'

The Hoopoe's sobs were echoed by other birds dotted about the field. Watt ignored them: 'Come on, you can tell us. Any information will be strictly confidential. Got you pinned down here, has he? Pinched your flight feathers? D'you want to press charges?'

'Hoo hoo.'

Watt's hand went to his pocket for his notebook. The Hoopoe flinched.

Swallow said, 'We're heading for England. I must get

there, or Princess Hiro will die. I'm going to fight the Prince of Darkness and overthrow him if I can. Then the Sun will come back into the world and the Swallows will come home.'

The Hoopoe looked at him for the first time. 'Oh, oh,' he sighed. 'Oh, if only you could. But look around you and you'll see what happens if you fail. We all tried to come home and he sentenced us to spend the rest of our lives here, in the Vale of Tears.'

'Vale of Tears?' said Watt disapprovingly. 'Seems to me that if you lot pulled yourselves together, this valley might be not half bad.'

'Hoo hoo, that's what makes it so miserable. It seems as if it could easily be better, but he makes us so wretched that every effort to improve things only makes it worse. And in the end we stay here and decay, because we can't think what else to do. Hoo hoo.'

'You could fly out,' suggested Swallow. Then he looked at Hoopoe's lack of feathers and added, 'It would be hard: but I'm sure it's possible.'

Hoopoe shook his head: 'He's taken our sense of direction. Whichever way we go, we find ourselves flying straight into his winds and they bring us back here.'

Watt wondered about paths through the woods, but again Hoopoe shook his head: 'They all lead back here. You set off down a path and after a couple of minutes you come to a cross-roads – it's always the same. And whichever turning you take brings you back here.'

Swallow's mind went back to the cross-roads which led 'out of the question'. Yes, this all had the mark of the Prince of Darkness. But nothing yet answered the question why the birds had decayed so quickly. Swallow felt embarrassed to ask, but he had to know. Hoopoe told him: 'We were all beautiful; and we brought that beauty into his world. He hates beauty. And he devised this prison so that we should decay and watch our beauty fall away.'

'Is there no remedy?'

'Only to overthrow him. But that's hoo-hoo-hopeless.' And Hoopoe burst out sobbing again.

'I shall defeat him,' said Swallow, 'with the help of Watt here. At least we'll try. But we must get some rest first. Can we stay here with you?'

'As far as I'm concerned, you can,' said Hoopoe. 'But I'll have to ask the others. You see, that's part of the punishment. If he gets wind of anyone resting, he doubles the misery of the others, which is why everyone's on their feet. Stay here, I'll have a word with them.'

And so saying, Hoopoe sobbed his way off across the field. The other birds heard him coming and dragged themselves to meet him.

Watt thought that this would take some time, and sat down on a little mound of grass. At once the cries and sobs from the far side of the field doubled in volume – 'Hoo hoo', 'Krornk', 'Wheet', 'Piou'.

Swallow turned to Watt: 'Look what you've done. Get up – quick!'

Watt did so. The noise subsided. And the exhausted, shattered birds went into a huddle. Scarcely a sign of life came from the group. It was almost as though, having drained themselves to get there, it was all they could do to stay and hear. No nodding of heads. No shifting of position. No voices raised in protest. Just the regular 'Hoo hoo hoo' of Hoopoe as he put the proposition; and an undercurrent of 'Crrr Crrr' from the Turtle Doves who, even in their misery, talked through the proceedings.

Then the meeting seemed to break up, apparently in disarray, for Hoopoe began the long trek back looking more crest-fallen than ever. When he had gone a few yards a mournful but commanding 'Krornk' stopped him in his tracks. He turned and rejoined the group. The new voice was that of the tall, drooping Heron who now, from his lofty eminence, addressed the clustered birds magisterially. They listened to him in silence, much as they had to Hoopoe, but somehow this silence seemed more respectful. Then he finished speaking; the birds dispersed; and Hoopoe and Heron made their painful way back across the field.

When at last they arrived, Hoopoe introduced Swallow and

Watt to Heron.

'How do you do?' said Watt, offering his hand.

'Not well – not well at all,' replied Heron, ignoring it, and looking at them out of weary, woebegone eyes.

Hoopoe explained that the first reaction to his proposal had been one of unanimous disapproval – no-one could stand a night of the misery that would entail. But then Heron had spoken up and said that anyone who came to challenge the Prince of Darkness must be helped, no matter what the cost – their last shred of self-respect demanded it. They had to help in any way they could. His arguments had prevailed. Swallow and Watt could stay; and Heron himself had offered to watch over them. Swallow marvelled how appearances could deceive, for from his bearing Heron looked completely cowed. But clearly within that battered, bedraggled shell, the old fighter's heart was still beating.

'Thank you very much,' he said.

'It is our duty,' replied Heron. 'If we can no longer fight, we must do what we can to help those who do. Mind you, if it's rest you're after, you'll not get a lot of it here. I'm afraid so long as you're here, trying to sleep, the cries from the rest of us will be pretty unbearable. Which is why I offered to stand guard. I suggest you plug your ears with moss and let me do your listening; otherwise you'll get no sleep at all.'

'That sounds like good thinking,' said Watt, looking round at the corner of the field for a suitable spot to stretch out. 'I'm for turning in right away. Not much difference between day and night here, and the sooner we've rested and on our way, the sooner your troubles will be over.'

Swallow agreed. Hoopoe sobbed. Heron nodded.

Hoopoe flapped off to brace himself for his misery, and Swallow and Watt went over to the corner, stuffing their ears with moss as they went. Watt stretched himself out on the ground, and Swallow found a suitable perch in the branches of a neighbouring tree.

At once through their ear-plugs they heard the cries of the birds fill the air with a great chorus of misery. And Swallow, as he listened from his branch, could have sworn it was raining from the heavy plop of raindrops which reached his ears. He looked out over the field and saw that the rain he heard was in fact the tears of the birds, pouring from their eyes and plummeting onto the already sodden ground.

Hoopoe had not been wrong when he called it the Vale of Tears.

# 12

# Rest in Peace

Resting, let alone sleeping, was not easy when one knew the price that was being paid. In the circumstances, however, Swallow saw that it was his duty to get what rest he could. He looked down at Watt, who had gone off as soon as his head touched the ground; and he envied him his capacity not to anticipate trouble, not to live through dangers until they happened. But, for better or worse, Swallows are not so uncomplicated; and as he settled himself to sleep, Swallow's head swam with the apprehension of what was to come.

He was to be 'dealt with in due course' – he knew that. But how? How was he to be dealt with? By decaying – like Hoopoe and the others? By exhaustion? Did the Prince of Darkness fuel himself on the energy others spent trying to reach him? That sounded very likely – but if so, was the answer to stop trying – in which case they would not reach their goal, and he would still get them in the end? Or was it to be by paralysis? By creeping fear? By battle? How? What horror, old or new, did his enemy have in store for him? He shook himself. The questions, though forward-looking, were futile: because even if, by chance, he hit on the right answer, the Prince (he felt sure) would simply change the question. Best try if he could to forget about the future and concentrate on the present. He was still there – that was something. And as long as he remained there, Princess Hiro and the others would be safe – that was something too. But how long would he be there? Tomorrow the future would be present. Tomorrow he would meet the Prince of Darkness, and the horror would be revealed. Tomorrow was 'do' and maybe 'die'; and if 'die' – then death too for Princess Hiro.

As he thought this the tear drops rang louder in his ears; the cries 'Hoo-hoo', 'Tree-tree-tree', 'Krornk' came closer and took on a different character. No longer were they the plaintive cries of birds in pain, but taunting, mocking laughter, harsh and cruel. He opened his eyes and saw that the birds had gathered beneath his tree. A visitor had arrived. They were clustered round it. They didn't seem to notice Swallow.

Hoopoe was speaking: 'Hoo-hoo-how do you do, little bird. Welcome to the Dark.'

Swallow craned his neck to see whom he was addressing, but the other birds got in the way.

'Such a pity your friends couldn't wait for you. But alas, they fell asleep, as soon as they got here – hoo-hoo – foolish creatures. Most unwise. They shouldn't have gone to sleep in the dark – not if they wanted to wake up again – hoo-hoo – such a pity.'

Swallow sensed that they were talking about him. 'I'm not asleep,' he cried, 'I'm here.' But no-one heard.

Hoopoe stepped back and Swallow was able to see the visitor: another Swallow – a tattered, moth-eaten Swallow. Hoopoe prodded it: 'What's the matter, little bird? Don't you like the dark? Are you afraid something unpleasant might happen? Are you? Well, I'm rather afraid it will – hoo-hoo . . .'

He put his head back and laughed, 'Hoo hoo hoo.'

Swallow saw his face and froze stiff with horror. For

instead of the sad features of Hoopoe, he found himself looking at the neat little face and bright saucer eyes of the Lemur.

The scales fell from Swallow's eyes and he saw the birds for what they really were. The Golden Oriole no longer hid his head in the grass. His head was held high now and sported the eye-patch and earring of the pirate, Alonso. The Turtle Doves puffed out their featherless pink breasts and revealed themselves as vicious winds who buffetted their victim remorselessly. The poor little Swallow edged away from them and into the clutches of the great gaunt Heron, who didn't even look much like a Heron any more. His feathers stood up angrily all over his head; and the bedraggled plumage covering his body was now instantly recognisable as the ragged clothing of the Wild Wind.

He grabbed the bird and held it in a vice-like grip. Swallow longed for Watt to stand up to him, or for Camel to come again to the rescue. But neither was anywhere to be seen.

'Sent your little friend to beard me in the desert, did you? Sent him sprouting orange trees, did you? What a shame he couldn't stay to watch you pay for his boldness . . . Krornk, Krornk.'

The winds gurgled appreciatively. Alonso bared his teeth in what he imagined to be a smile. And the Lemur, great saucer eyes shining in the dark, laughed in the little bird's face, 'Hoo hoo hoo.' The bird strained away from him, and in doing so looked straight at Swallow with mutely appealing, deep, beautiful, immeasurably sad eyes.

Swallow gasped. Those eyes – he would know them anywhere! It was his Princess! His beautiful, sweet, innocent Princess! What had they done to her? What were they doing to her? He had to stop them. He strove to get up; but he wasn't sitting down. He tried to move forward; the effort was in vain. He flapped his wings; as in a vacuum. He screamed his defiance: 'You brutes! You bullies! I'll be even with you!' But no sound came.

The Lemur laughed; the winds gurgled; Alonso showed his teeth; and the Wild Wind tightened his grip on the Princess.

All Swallow could see now was her limp tail twitching; all he could hear was the heavy plop of her tears on the dark, dank floor.

Then the darkness deepened behind them. They fell silent and turned towards it. For a moment all was quiet. A shadow separated itself from the rest of the darkness and glided across the field towards them. It stopped by a tree stump a few yards away. Swallow looked and looked again for the cause of the shadow; but saw nothing, no substance, just the shadow. He felt its presence though; and he knew what it wanted – his Princess. The Wild Wind knew too, and carried her struggling across to the shadow.

Swallow was seized by a fearful trembling, brought on by knowledge that he would happily have been without: knowledge that the shadow would speak; and that when it did he would recognise the voice.

Sure enough the shadow spoke on cue: 'Come, Princess. You are to be my bride.'

And Swallow did recognise the voice. How could he not? It had been with him ever since he entered the jungle – the voice from the shadows, the voice of the Prince of Darkness. He had shadowed them, had shadowed the greater part of the world; and now he was about to shadow the Princess.

'No!' he cried. 'No! No!'

No-one heard.

The Wind held the Princess tight. The voice continued: 'Many creatures wish to marry the Prince of Darkness. But only one is worthy: she who hates him with every fibre of her being, she who will die every minute in his presence. She is to be my bride. You, Princess! You! Put her down.'

The Wind placed the struggling Princess on the tree-stump, then withdrew. She sat as if glued, looking all about for help. No-one moved.

She squirmed, trying to free herself. 'Help! Help!' The shadow swelled behind her.

Swallow tried desperately to break out of his own imprisonment.

'Hoo hoo', 'Krornk', 'Took'.

The shadow fell over her tail. She strained away from it.

'Crr crr.'

Swallow tore at his invisible chains.

The shadow crept up to her legs.

Swallow tore again and ripped out several feathers.

Now her breast was in shadow.

He tore again, removed more feathers, and found himself free. He launched himself forward, knocking the Lemur and the Wind out of the way.

Now her crop. Only her head remained.

He hurled himself forward to cover her before the shadow did.

A voice sounded in his ear: 'Careful! Careful! Blimey – what's going on?'

Swallow sat up, blinking in the grey light, and saw that the Princess he had been saving, was, in fact, Watt, who didn't take kindly to such attentions. He got up and brushed himself down. Swallow rose too. The mournful cries and sobbing subsided. He removed his ear-plugs and looked round the field. Everything was as it had been when they went to sleep: Heron stood guard, and the other birds, scattered round the field were much as before. Had it been a dream, then? Or a premonition? There was only one way to find out: they must be on their way. Today was the day and now the hour – now, while they were fresh and rested – to meet the Prince of Darkness.

He went across to thank Heron.

'Krornk. Glad to have been of help – krornk. But I can't say I'm sorry you've woken. That was the most miserable night I've spent in years.'

'Hoo hoo hoo, you can say that again,' added Hoopoe.

'Let's hope it was worth it,' said Swallow.

'Krornk – just do your best. That's all we ask. Now, off you go, before you lose heart.'

Swallow turned to Watt: 'Ready?' Watt nodded and climbed aboard.

'Goodbye and thank you.' Swallow flapped his wings and up they soared.

'Hoo hoo, good luck,' called Hoopoe. 'Krornk krornk,' cried Heron.

Then they were gone, engulfed once more in their misery; and Swallow and Watt were on their way.

# 13

# When Friends Fall Out

They now passed through a ghostly land. The light had become so dim, the greyness so dense, that they saw nothing clearly – just vague shapes which loomed up at them, threatened briefly, then passed harmlessly by. The swelling shadow of his dream was still fresh in Swallow's memory, and he expected each of these to turn into the Prince of Darkness. Yet he faced the prospect with a strange new fatalism. They had come so far; there had been so many enemies. It was almost good to know that this was it at last – the big test and then no more.

Watt's homing instinct locked onto its target. He was like a policeman possessed, and clasped Swallow tightly round the throat with one hand, while with the other he pointed into the dense grey fog ahead: 'That way'. And Swallow had no hesitation in following his directions. Come what may: come England, come the Prince of Darkness, as far as he was concerned, they could not arrive a moment too soon.

They raced now. The exhaustion of the previous day had fallen away, and the knowledge that this was indeed the last lap called forth unsuspected reserves of energy in Swallow.

On and on they flew. The greyness became ever thicker and darker, until it was greyness no more, but blackness – a wall of blackness and they were in the middle of it. Swallow could no longer see Watt's finger pointing the way, so Watt changed his directions to 'Left a bit', 'Right a bit', 'Straight ahead'. On and on. Growing weary. No sign of the Prince of Darkness. No sign of England. 'Straight ahead.' On and on, his wings getting heavy. Still no sign.

'Are you sure you've got the route right?' asked Swallow.

'Straight ahead,' repeated Watt.

On and on. His reserves of energy draining away. Watt beginning to seem like a dead weight. Swallow's speed now dropping – fifty, forty, thirty, twenty miles an hour. Still no sign. Where was he? Where was the Prince of Darkness? If he wanted to meet them, here they were! 'Come on! Come and get us!' Swallow wanted to shout; and would have shouted had he had strength left to do so. But just at that moment he began to see what their enemy was up to, and was glad that he had said nothing. He wondered that he had not seen it before: it was the way the dark behaved the world over. When the Sun was at its height, the dark hid. But as soon as the Sun showed signs of weakening, the shadows lengthened and the dark came creeping out of its secret places and took over. And, as with the dark, so too with the Prince of Darkness. Wasn't it foolish to suppose that he would agree to meet a fresh, well-rested foe, eager for the fray? He who knew so much? Who had shadowed them so much of the way? Was perhaps shadowing them even now? Last night he had known they were there, but had let them rest. Why? Obviously because he wasn't ready to meet them. He wanted a weak, divided foe. He would let them wear themselves out trying to find him, let them, in their desire to destroy him, destroy themselves. And then, when they were exhausted, when they had begun to fall out with each other, then he would make his entrance.

Very well. If that was what he wanted, that was what they would give him: a weak, divided foe. They must give the appearance of being exhausted and at odds while they still had some strength and some wit left.

At least, Swallow must. This time Watt would have to be left in the dark, so to speak. That way he would play his part more convincingly. Swallow felt guilty about this, but he knew that if was to deceive his enemy – particularly this all-seeing, all-hearing enemy – it was vital that he deceive his friend as well. And there could be no half measures: Watt (and anyone else who might be watching) must be left in no doubt that the friendship was at an end. Swallow just prayed that for once he had got it right and that someone else *was* watching; because if they were not – he thought the unthinkable – if they were not, he would shortly have Watt's death on his conscience.

He slowed down still further. Nineteen, eighteen, seventeen miles an hour, flapping his wings feebly. They began to lose height.

'What's the matter?' asked Watt.

'I'm exhausted,' Swallow snapped back. 'What do you think?'

'It can't be far now,' Watt pleaded. 'Come on. Just a little bit more.'

'Can't be far. Can't be far,' Swallow muttered, almost to himself, 'that's all I ever hear from you . . . But we don't get there, do we?'

'We will. I promise, we will.'

Sixteen miles an hour. Fifteen.

'I suppose you think it's fun carrying you all this way?'

'What?'

'I could have been there by now . . . If I hadn't had you to carry. *And* I could have chosen my own route – which would have saved a lot of trouble.'

'But we're working together – as a team. I steer, you fly. That was the arrangement, wasn't it?'

Fourteen.

'Well, wasn't it?'

'Yes – it was. But . . . it wasn't part of the plan – not of my plan anyway – that you should steer us into trouble.'

'I haven't. I've directed you to England. I never said I could do anything else.'

Twelve. Losing height all the time.

'I shouldn't be surprised to find you were put there by the Prince of Darkness to slow me down.'

'You can't think that. Not after all we've been through. You can't! You can't!'

Ten miles an hour.

'We're not going to make it.'

'We are. We must.'

'Maybe – but not together.'

'What?'

'Together we haven't a chance. On my own I might still make it.'

'What are you talking about?'

'I'm saying that this is where we part company. You've held me back for too long. From now on . . .'

Swallow started to roll over on to his side. Watt clung to him for dear life: 'No, Swallow! No, no!'

'. . . you're on your own.' Swallow rolled completely upside down and threw Watt off into the darkness.

'No! No, Swallow! I'm your friend . . . I'm your . . .' he cried. But in a moment he was gone.

Swallow struggled on alone. He knew that he had to make it look good. He flew with new purpose now; raised his speed again to fifteen, even twenty miles an hour, climbed a little, kept going with grim determination. But his face showed the strain of a final effort, an effort he could not keep up for long. All at once it became too much. The strength seemed to go from his wings. He was dropping again, faster and faster with every second, until all forward movement had ceased and he was falling like a stone.

'Now,' he thought. 'Now is the time to meet the Prince of Darkness. Come on. Come on – wherever you are. I'm here. Come and get me!'

But it wasn't to be.

Swallow fell until he hit the water. The splash burst on his eardrums like an explosion, and the chill of the black northern water pierced him to the marrow. His senses were numbed.

The world receded. The blackness faded. And then there was nothing.

# 14

# The Enemy Appears

The Prince of Darkness watched as the limp little body floated down through the water and came to rest on the ocean bed a few feet from where he was standing. He turned to his companion. 'Excellent,' he said, 'excellent. You did well.'

Watt made no reply.

'Oh, come now,' the Prince continued, reading his thoughts. 'He threw you off, didn't he? Pitched you out into the darkness? That shows how much he valued your friendship.'

Watt gave a sigh. 'If only he'd trusted me, we'd have made it. I'm sure we would.'

'Nonsense. It was precisely because he trusted you that he didn't make it – as he eventually realised – though too late to do him any good. Silly little bird! To think that he could get the better of me!'

'We beat all the others,' said Watt.

'Only because I let you. I like to see my underlings get beaten every so often. It stops them getting out of hand. Still, fair's fair – you did very well. Better than I expected, to be quite candid with you. But it's a different matter overcoming enemies you can see, from trying to tackle the one you never see; who's always near but always out of reach; the enemy who only becomes visible when you stop looking. I refer, of course, to myself. Now, how do you fight an enemy like that, eh? Eh? You don't, do you? You give up and serve him. As you have done.'

'I never said I'd serve you.'

'My dear fellow, of course you didn't. But then *you* didn't have to, did you? In your case it should have been obvious from the start - even to you. You were dug up out of the darkness underground; and you're bound for England, which is in the very heart of my dominions. What else could you be but my servant?'

'What if I refuse?'

'You can't. You're a policeman. Policemen enforce the law. And in England at the moment I make the law. So, you serve me: you have no choice in the matter.'

Watt's mind boggled. He accepted the argument, but resisted the conclusion. He was still very much a creature of instinct, and his instinct told him this was wrong. But it didn't tell him why. He wished he was older, that his brain had developed and could work it out. He wished Swallow were there to advise him. But it hadn't and he wasn't, and all Watt could do was to rehearse the argument, like a spider endlessly spinning a web, in the hope that some fly of illumination would settle on it. He was an English policeman; he had English law in his brain; and so long as the Prince of Darkness ruled in England, English law was his law and Watt *should* feel happy to be his servant.

He should, but he didn't. He *couldn't.*

The Prince, thought-reading again, went on. 'You see, that's the trouble with having values: you can be trapped in them. Little Swallow there, he had values - courage, trust, loyalty - wonderful values. I wouldn't say a word against them. He believed in being loyal to his friends - so I gave him a friend and he was loyal to him. And the friend brought him right into my hands without my having to raise a finger. Ha, ha! Fiendish, isn't it? Ha, ha!'

And so saying he turned away to bask in the plaudits of his minions in the Great Hall. They cackled their appreciation of their master's diabolical cleverness.

To say that the hall was 'Great' is to give it a name, but such a phrase does not adequately describe it. Watt's limited powers of description were stretched to the uttermost. It was not like anything he had ever seen before or (to make it somewhat more exceptional since he hadn't as yet seen a great deal) that he ever expected to see again. For a start it was carved out of water. No bricks, no stones held it up, just the water itself, which stood there as in a whirlpool, caught between two opposing forces: the evil which repelled it, and its own weight which pressed in upon it. Caught thus it stood there like the stoutest stone palace. Great fluted columns of water rose sheer, a hundred feet up from the sea bed, then branched out to support an ornately carved water roof. At one end a huge gothic doorway framed heavy water doors, and the other end was given over entirely to an enormous stained-water window, wherein were depicted the legendary triumphs of the Dark: the day-long eclipse of the Sun, when the Prince of Darkness had first rebelled; the Famous Flood, with Noah cast as a smiling, sunlit villain, foiling the triumph of the dark water creatures; and the Black Blindness – perhaps the cleverest campaign yet waged by the Prince – for when all were blind, what would it matter how the Sun shone – darkness would rule everywhere.

The hall was lit by torches which burnt black against the walls and sent out shafts of black light. And in this unwholesome glow, Watt saw them. They were all there, all the servants of darkness whom he and Swallow had met and overcome: the Black Mamba, swinging a length of creeper and looking venomous; the Wild Wind of the Sahara, surrounded as always by his troops, puffing himself up to assert his importance, the little Lemur, beautiful costume scuffed and torn, eyes bright, round and piercing, darting hatred at Watt; and many more creatures of the Dark. Severe-looking Owls and red-eyed Bats thronged the galleries. Deep-water Fishes peered through the walls. Great greasy bulbous Toads stood guard on the doors. And in the body of the hall there wriggled Worms, masses of them – Glow Worms, Tape

Worms, Lug Worms, Silk Worms, Flat Worms, Round Worms, Ring Worms – all kow-towing to their leader and rejoicing in his power.

And there was the Prince of Darkness himself – not at all as one would have imagined. He was a Prince, there could be no mistaking that – his garments proclaimed it. But he wasn't big; he wasn't black; he didn't swell like the shadow of Swallow's dream. On the contrary, he was small, thin, absolutely white – almost translucent. He looked fragile and sickly, like a flower that has grown in the dark – full of a thrusting power, but without health, without well-being. It was as though his sense of deprivation had turned him sour. He wanted the light, but couldn't reach it; and not having it, he hated it and would not rest until all others hated it with him.

His white clothes were edged with liquid jewels; and on his head he wore a crown, black as jet, made (he told Watt) from the black gold at the earth's centre, and encrusted with dark gems. Everything that could reflect – jewels, crown, eyes and teeth – shone black, mirroring the surrounding pitch. He was magnificently repellent: his image embedded itself in the mind and waking or sleeping was not to be erased.

But how did Watt come to be here, in this presence, in this hall? He had no idea. All he knew was that no sooner had Swallow tossed him off his back into the void, than he had found himself here, in this palace on the ocean floor, beside this creature who claimed to be his master.

And now the Prince and his cohorts were cackling over their victory. Watt felt a very unpolicemanly fury rising within him. He crossed quickly behind the Prince, drawing out his truncheon as he did so. He was only a pace away, with the truncheon aiming a scything blow at the back of the Prince's legs, when he stopped dead. He dropped the truncheon. His hands clutched his head. He fell to the ground and lay there, writhing. Inside his head all was black and swollen. Outside, his eyes bulged, his ears popped, his mouth puffed out. His head felt like a septic boil about to burst – whenever it touched anything the pain was indescribable and made him shoot here and there like a squib. The scene was watched with rapt, delighted attention by the court, but of that Watt knew nothing. All he knew was the pain inside his head.

The Prince's voice penetrated through the pain: 'You mustn't hit me. After all, I've broken no law. I simply let your little friend die trying to find me. Now, I can hardly be blamed for that, can I? I never asked him to come.'

The voice stopped; and as if to hammer the point home, the pain surged to new peaks, so acute that they all but lifted Watt off the ground in his agony, and the audience off their feet in ecstasy. Then it vanished and Watt's head cleared. He looked up to see the Prince stifle his courtiers' hilarity with a peremptory gesture, and then order two of the Toads to bring Swallow's body into the hall. They bowed their acknowledgement and retreated to the wall of water. Once there, they laid their pikes against the wall and dived in. They swam over to Swallow. One grabbed his wings, the other his tail, and they dragged him back and dumped him unceremoniously at their master's feet. They then withdrew discreetly to their posts on the doors, collecting their pikes on the way.

The Prince spread his arms wide and the court bowed their heads. The silence took on an awful, ominous solemnity. All eyes were shut except Watt's and the Prince's. The Prince looked down at his victim. He seemed for a moment to forget where he was, to lose himself in contemplation of his fallen enemy. Then, as if disembodied, his voice rang out, high and thrilling.

'So end all who oppose the Prince of Darkness.'

'So end all,' echoed the courtiers.

'I am everywhere. I am invincible.'

'He is invincible,' came the response.

'My enemies see only my shadows. They chase them; they run from them, they cannot escape them. And whichever way they go, my enemies run to me.'

'His enemies run to him.'

'My shadows go where they will. The Sun cannot dispel them.'

'The Sun cannot dispel them.'

'The brighter the light, the sharper my shadows. They will pierce through the light and poison the Sun.'

'They will poison the Sun.'

'Then the world will be shadowed and my day will come.'

'His day will come.'

'When the dark and the light will once more be one.'

'One. Dark One, Dark One. Hail, Dark One! Hail, Dark One!'

The hall rang to the rising chant. The water roof rippled as though wanting to escape, and the panes of the window shook with the evil vibrations. The Prince stood there, arms wide, exultant for a few seconds, before turning again to Watt.

'Come here,' he said.

Watt got up and crossed to him.

'You were very fond of this little bird, weren't you? No, don't deny it. I can tell. And I suppose you're sad now that he's dead, eh? It's understandable. But you needn't be, you know. Because now I will bring him back to life.'

Watt's heart leapt. Perhaps his instinct had been wrong. Perhaps the Prince was not the monster he had thought him. The Prince continued: 'I'm going to let my Maggots eat him. That way, you see, my enemy becomes my servant; and you, instead of having one useless dead friend, will have hundreds of little live ones. There now, aren't I kind?' He smiled; the court applauded; Watt's heart fell.

'Perhaps that will teach you to keep your emotions under control. You will stay here with your "friend" until it is dinner time. Then you will watch my Maggots feast themselves upon him. And any that's left over you may eat, what? Wouldn't want you to go hungry, would we? Ha, ha.'

He laughed in Watt's face, then turned on his heel and strode from the hall. His courtiers, giggling and spluttering, snaked out in a long line behind him.

When the last of them had gone, the heavy doors banged to. The sound reverberated round the hall for a while, fading gradually. Then all was still. For the first time in his life, Watt came to a stop. He felt like a clockwork toy that has fallen on its side, wheels whirring, going nowhere. He moved over to

Swallow and looked down at him. Poor Swallow. To have come so far and come to this. While they had been on the move, Watt had never considered the enormity of their task. But now that they'd stopped, he acquired for the first time a sense of the disproportion. There they were, the two of them, insignificant specks in this huge vault, where he could bellow at the top of his voice and it would sound like a Mouse in a cathedral, and they had taken on the Prince of Darkness and all his forces. Poor Swallow . . . Poor silly Swallow . . . silly to take on something so far beyond him . . . But then – something must have fired him to it – some . . . passion. Passion – that was something Watt knew very little about. He hoped to one day, but as yet it was outside his experience. Perhaps passion could transform small creatures into heroes – maybe it had transformed Swallow – because strangely enough, Watt had never doubted Swallow's ability to reach his goal . . . never . . . until now when he'd failed . . . now when he was . . . No. Passion just confused things. Silly Swallow – better off without it . . . might still be alive . . . But then – if Swallow hadn't had it, perhaps they would never have met . . . and then they'd have missed all those good times together. Watt thought of hurtling down the corridor before the swirling blackness; seeing off Alonso and his comrades; waking up in the Vale of Tears to find Swallow saving him from heaven knew what horror; the satisfaction of kicking the Mamba off his branch. Yes – that had been good. He went through the motion again, and felt again the pleasing slap of snake flesh against his boot. He looked down and saw that he was kicking Swallow. He withdrew his foot guiltily and wandered across to the wall of water. He looked out to the spot where Swallow had first floated down. He ran his finger down the wall, as down a wet window pane, and it pierced through the surface and into the water outside. A thought came to him. The Toads had dived through the wall. He had seen them. Then what was to stop him doing the same? Diving in and swimming off with Swallow's body to some place where no-one would find them, where Swallow could rest in peace, and he might die undisturbed? Nothing as far as he could see.

He moved quickly back to Swallow, picked up the little body and returned with it to the wall. He stopped for a second, took a deep breath, and dived in. His head smashed into the wall with an impact which crumpled his helmet. Swallow was thrown from his arms. And Watt sank, with the Prince's laughter ringing in his poor bruised brain, to the floor.

How long he lay there he couldn't say. Maybe minutes. More likely hours. He was finally roused by a sharp pain in his side. He opened his eyes to see two Toads ballooning over him, prodding him with their pikes. They motioned him to get up, then forced him across the hall to the spot in the centre where Swallow was now laid out. Watt feared the worst; and when, a few moments later, the heavy doors swung open and a troop of Trencher Maggots marched in, his fears were realised. Each Maggot shouldered a knife and fork, and bore on his arm a plate-shield. They marched down the hall and came to a halt in two lines, one either side of Swallow. The Toads poked Watt forward to stand by Swallow's head.

The Maggots wasted no time, but set to work at once. They were very methodical. First they emptied Swallow's pockets, determined not to overlook any tit-bits. But finding nothing that appealed, they abandoned the objects they found there, and returned to their main course. The precious items that had helped Swallow and Watt come so far – the orange seeds, the little bottle of magic water, and a strange hour-glass that Watt hadn't seen before – all lay discarded and disregarded on the floor.

This couldn't be right. They hadn't come this far for Watt to be a spectator at his friend's dismemberment. That had to be wrong.

The Maggots sharpened their knives and tucked their napkins in at their collars. Watt searched for his brain in order to rack it. There must be something he could do. He felt, in some strange way, as though Swallow – though dead – were relying on him. But if so the reliance was misplaced, for he had no answer.

The Maggots put away their sharpeners and bowed their

heads in prayer. Watt stared empty-headed at the hour-glass. The sands seemed to have stuck in the neck – every now and then one would fall through. It fascinated him. One fell.

The chief Maggot led his troops in grace: 'For what we are about to receive . . .'

Watt pondered. If Swallow was dead, the Maggots had a perfect right to eat him – to deny them that was to deny their right to exist.

Another grain of sand fell.

The Maggots approached their dinner. The Toads forced Watt forward with their pikes.

Watt didn't deny their right to exist. He didn't. But . . .

The Maggots crawled all over Swallow, sawing at his flesh with their sharp little knives.

. . . but he couldn't watch. Watt turned away. He would rather impale himself on the Toads' pikes.

Another grain fell.

His big policeman's boot knocked the little bottle of magic water and sent it clattering across the floor. The stopper worked loose and a spray of the water arched over Swallow and the salivating Maggots.

It landed with a conventional enough rain-like patter. But that was all that was conventional. For what happened after was so unexpected (and to some unwelcome), that an impartial observer might be forgiven for thinking that what he next heard was the unmistakable sound of tables turning.

# 15

# The Prince Does His Worst

Watt, who was by no means an impartial observer, heard a hissing and spitting behind him, like the sound of water dropped onto hot fat. He turned to see what the noise was, then held his nose and screwed up his eyes as a cloud of poisonous, acrid fumes enveloped him. He remained in this posture for some time unable to look, scarcely even able to breathe. Then the smoke thinned sufficiently for him to open his eyes, and what he saw caused him to open his mouth, which admitted the lingering smoke down his throat and caused him to close both eyes and mouth again and to choke briefly. But what he had seen remained imprinted on the backs of his eyes, and as soon as he was able he looked again for confirmation – this time, however, clamping his mouth tight shut, and his eyes goggling by way of compensation, as though the sight which greeted them was too much to be admitted by any ordinary organs. As indeed it was.

*Swallow was alive!* He sat there fresh, alert, ready for action – like a Cat roused by an enemy from its slumber. However wide Watt opened his eyes, he could not believe them. Swallow had been dead. Rhino had said nothing about the water raising from the dead. And raising from the dead in more ways than one, for all around Swallow lay fallen Maggots, dead or dying. The water that had landed on them had had precisely the opposite effect to that on Swallow. They were creatures of the dark and hated light; therefore the water, being the essence of light, had annihilated them. It had burnt through their flesh, shrinking and shrivelling them and giving off the odious vapours that had engulfed Watt. Watt stood there, metaphorically open-mouthed at least, for a long moment.

The Toads too were flabbergasted and forgot about Watt as they rivetted their attention to the newly-revived Swallow. One of the guards on the doors sounded the alarm. With enviable presence of mind Swallow threw off the few mesmerised Maggots that still clung to him, and collected his belongings. Watt broke out of his trance and, though still doubting the evidence of his senses, followed Swallow's example by moving over to pick up the little bottle. There was not much water left, but it was clearly so powerful that even a drop might be vital.

Before he could replace the stopper the Prince and his retinue appeared in the doorway. Watt stood still, bottle uncorked in his hand. Swallow scrambled to his feet. The Maggots hissed and howled. The Prince's smile hung forgotten on his face; but behind it he was livid and, for perhaps the first time in his being, a little afraid. His skin yellowed slightly as he gaped at Swallow. The bird was alive! The bird who had been seeking him; who had defeated one after another of his lieutenants; whom he had seen to be dead, or else would never have admitted to his presence. That bird stood before him, alive, well and, apart from the cuts made by the Maggots' knives, unscathed.

'What's going on?' he demanded.

Watt confessed: 'I . . . er . . . spilt some of this water over him . . . and, er . . .'

'Let me see,' said the Prince, reaching for the bottle.

Watt held it out to him.

'Don't touch it! Don't touch it!' came the plaintive Maggot chorus. 'Look what happened to us.'

The Prince looked and saw the wounded Maggots still frizzing on the floor. He withdrew his hand.

Watt held the bottle out at arm's length as though afraid of what it might do to him. 'What shall I do with it?' he asked.

'Keep it out of his reach,' replied his master, indicating Swallow. 'And don't spill any more.'

Watt hammered down the stopper and put the bottle in his

pocket for safety.

The Prince regained the appearance at least of composure and turned to Swallow: 'I believe you've been looking for me?'

'Not you. England,' said Swallow. 'England is my home. I was going back there – would have got there too, if it hadn't been for him.'

These words were directed at Watt, who would have protested had not the Prince forestalled him: 'Yes – thoughtful of me, wasn't it? – to give you a little friend. He's really finding it quite hard adjusting to the fact that he's my servant.'

'I don't know why he should, he's always done everything you wanted.'

'Just what I tell him,' chortled the Prince.

Swallow went on: 'Well, I mean to get to England. I don't want to fight you, but if I must, I must.'

'What a brave little bird,' the Prince simpered. 'No, I'm sure fighting won't be necessary. Fisticuffs and all that sort of thing really isn't my style. I prefer . . . gentle persuasion. I do wish you'd try to see things from my point of view, you know. I have a kingdom to rule. I simply cannot allow any Tom-Tit or Swallow to come along and cock a snook at my authority.'

'You had a kingdom before,' said Swallow, 'which no-one tried to take from you. You had the night, the underground, the waters, and hundreds of creatures willing to serve you. Why couldn't you be content?'

'Divine discontent, I suppose. I felt I could be so much better than I was – a slight extension of my kingdom and I could be all-powerful. Terribly tempting. Besides I got fed up being pushed around and made to feel inferior. How would you like it if every day you were shoved out of the way just as the world was beginning to sit up and take notice? You wouldn't like it, would you? Well, no more do I. And since it seems I am not to be given my due while the light is around, the light will just have to be extinguished, so you can all learn to love the dark.'

'Never!' cried Swallow. 'I will never do that. Darkness is

evil. You make creatures miserable. You delight in causing pain and suffering.'

'I delight in justice. And it is justice and no more to make those suffer, who persist in loving the light.'

He smiled at Swallow. And, as he did, Swallow had the strange feeling that something was trying to enter, to take possession of him – much as the thoughts had done earlier. But this time he seemed to be protected. His flesh tingled, his vision blurred and dimmed. He saw as through a pall of smoke, but he saw. He saw the Prince's fixed smile, intent, unchanging. He saw the evil eyes straining to pierce through to his soul. He had no idea what the Prince was up to, but whatever it was, it was not meant to do him good. He must resist.

He breathed his defiance: 'Well, I love the light. And always will. So there. What are you going to do about that?'

As he spoke his vision cleared. The Prince still smiled, but Swallow thought, just for a moment, that he saw a flicker of uncertainty behind the smiling eyes.

'Dear, dear, dear,' said the Prince, gazing round his court in well-simulated dismay, 'braved in my own court! Whatever next? Well, what should we do with you, eh? Return you to the Vale of Tears? Give you to the Mamba?'

The Mamba's eyes, hooded hitherto in the presence of his master, glowed again with something of their old fire. He twirled the creeper with evil intent.

'No, no. Such a victory would prove nothing. Others would follow in your footsteps, stirred by your example. No, I have a better idea. I will undertake to prove to you that darkness is preferable to light. And if I succeed, you will become my servant and help to spread my kingdom throughout the world. What do you say?'

Watt prayed that Swallow would refuse the challenge. He had watched the foregoing with a mixture of emotions: fear and amazement very much predominated, but hope was also just there and some faint beginnings of understanding – particularly of the power of the Prince's shadows. He had seen the Prince smile at Swallow, and had seen at the same time several shadows (including Swallow's own) rise up and envelop him like a cloak. He realised that it must have been some such process that had recently caused him such agony, when the blackness entered his brain. But Swallow miraculously seemed to be immune from the shadows' power, for though they remained wrapped about him, they were evidently unable to enter, and the moment he spoke they abandoned the attempt and reverted to normal. 'Round One to Swallow,' thought Watt. But he sensed that they were now entering Round Two; there was no knowing what tricks the Prince would have up his sleeve; and Watt prayed for Swallow to refuse the challenge.

For Swallow, however, there was no choicc. This was his test: he had to stand up to the Prince of Darkness and defeat him on his own terms, or he wouldn't deserve to get to England.

'Very well,' he replied. 'If you can prove that darkness is preferable to light, I will embrace the Darkness as now I love light.'

'Spoken like a champion,' said the Prince. 'Oh, this *is* going to be fun! Are you ready?'

Swallow nodded.

'Right. Off we go.'

Without further preamble he lunged at Swallow with his first argument: 'The dark came first and so is best.'

This was no more than an opening thrust and Swallow had no difficulty parrying it. 'My father came before me,' he replied, 'and was in his day as I am in mine. Neither better nor worse.'

'The dark makes things grow,' said the Prince.

'But the light makes them blossom.'

'Without the seed to grow in the dark, you would have no blossom.'

'And without the fruit ripened in the light, you would have no seed.'

The Prince changed his tack: 'You came out of the dark and to dark you shall return.'

'I came into the light and in light I shall remain.'

'You seek refuge with me at the end of every day, for what is sleep but flight into darkness?'

'Rather flight from darkness, for in sleep I inhabit the day of my dreams.'

The Prince began to be in earnest. Small beads of sweat formed on his brow and trickled down his nose. What was the matter with this blessed bird? Whenever he tried these aphorisms on his courtiers, they seemed unanswerable. He went on, his face tightening, the veins standing out under the rim of his crown: 'Without the dark, light is nothing.'

'On the contrary, dark is nothing but an absence of light.'

The Prince saw an opening and dived in: 'How can that be, if dark existed first?'

'Because dark is denial. In itself it is not. It hates and destroys whatever is. While there is light, it denies that. But take the light away and dark will still deny. Only then it will deny itself – destroy itself.'

'Nonsense! Nonsense! I deny nothing. I affirm. I am positive. I am!'

Again the smile. Again Swallow's vision blurred and again he forced himself to keep talking: 'Before time was . . . what was it . . . dark or light?'

On the instant, his vision cleared. And as it did, he saw once more the uncertainty behind the smile. Only this time there was no doubt. It was the Prince's turn to think. There was a catch in the question. He knew it; but he didn't know how to avoid it. He didn't want to say it had been dark, but to say something else was to admit the primacy of light. 'Dark, of course,' he replied.

Swallow pinned him with his admission: 'And before time was, nothing was. Therefore dark is nothing. It is not.'

The Prince's followers began to shift uneasily. But their master was not so easily beaten: 'If so, the Creator created out of nothing: and he created in his own image, which was therefore dark.'

'Did the Creator then, create nothing?'

'No, of course . . .'

'Then he created *something*. And since, as agreed, dark is

nothing, he must have created light. And the world, being created, is a light world. And I and all other creatures in it are creatures of the light. You are the intruder. Your world is elsewhere.'

The stirrings among the courtiers mounted to a distinct rumbling of discontent. What was this? Their master, the Prince of Darkness, being put down by a wretched Swallow? They itched to get at him. And the Prince, knowing that to stand idly by was to lose control of his followers, again changed tack abruptly.

'I will set you a problem,' he said. 'If you solve it, England is yours and I will abandon my efforts to take over the world. But if you fail, you are to serve me. Agreed?'

'Agreed.'

The rumblings subsided. The Prince called Watt over and whispered in his ear. Watt nodded. The Prince turned back to Swallow. 'In that wall you will see two doors. One leads to England, the other to everlasting darkness. You must choose which door to go through; and to help you make your choice, you may ask either me or your friend here one question, to which the answer will be 'Yes' or 'No'. One of us will tell the truth, the other will lie. Do you understand?'

'Yes,' said Swallow. 'I understand.'

'Very well. You have two minutes. Starting from . . . *now!*'

Swallow thought; his brow furrowed, his mind raced. Which door? Which door? How was he to choose? He could ask one question. But which? There seemed to be so many – none of them askable, for they would all leave him needing to ask another. One question – to which one would answer truthfully and the other would lie – that would tell him which door. It didn't sound possible. 'One minute, forty-five seconds,' said the Prince.

Swallow knew there was an answer. But where? He'd heard this kind of question before. Down in the south in the long hot evenings the elders were always puzzling over this sort of thing. Only he had never had any time for it. Now alas he had time to repent his light-headedness. He asked himself futilely, 'Who would be most likely to tell the truth?' And returned himself the frustrating answer: 'Watt, of course – unless he'd been told to lie.' In that case he would do as he was told, for it wasn't in his nature to break rules, even bad ones. Then it seemed that he couldn't know who was telling the truth; and that meant he would have to find a question to which the answer would be the same – truth or lie.

'One minute, thirty seconds.'

Whenever the Prince called out the time, Swallow's brain clouded with panic and he lost precious seconds. A question to which the answer was the same – truth or lie? Let's see. *If I ask you whether the right-hand door leads to England, and you answer "Yes", will you be lying?*

Come on Swallow. Come on! Work it out! It's something like that. If he's lying and he answers 'Yes', that means 'No – he *wouldn't* be lying if he said "Yes that was the door to England".' But . . . but he's bound to lie. So he must be lying now; *and* he must have been lying then. In other words he can't answer the question. And if he's telling the truth and says 'Yes', that means he *would be* lying if he said that was the door . . . But he's bound to tell the truth: he couldn't be lying.

He found himself staring vacantly at the Prince, waiting for the next time check. It wasn't long in coming.

'One minute.'

Watt tried to will Swallow to find the answer, or failing that, to open a door. After all, he had a fifty-fifty chance of being right. But think what hung on it – their future, the Swallows' future, the world's future. Open the wrong door even an inch and everlasting darkness would pour out and cover the world. Then who would care about a Vale of Tears, or sand castles in the Sahara? The whole world would be laid waste.

Swallow tried to keep hold of the question he'd formed. It was so nearly right. If he could alter it just a little, he'd be there. He couldn't ask the truth-teller if he had been lying, because he couldn't lie. Nor could he ask the liar a question which involved him telling the truth, because that too was out of bounds. And yet the question must somehow balance truth and lie so that the answer, no matter who was asked, would be the same.

*If I were to ask you, whether the left-hand door leads to England... and you answer 'Yes' – would that be...*

'Thirty seconds.'

Oh, wait a minute! Wait a minute! You've made me lose it now. *If I asked you...* An image flashed across his brain, blocking his thought. Suspecting a trick he tried to push it away. *If I asked you...* The image formed again. It was his Princess. She was talking to him. He wiped out the image. Not now! *If I asked you...* Again the image. Again the attempted wiping.

'Twenty seconds.'

*If I asked you... If I asked you...* What? What did he want to ask? He'd forgotten the question. *If I asked you...* There again was the image, forcing its way into his brain, speaking to him. Despairing, he listened: *Ask him what the other would answer.*

'Ten seconds.'

*Ask him what the other...*

With a flash of realisation, Swallow saw that his Princess was telling him what he had been trying to formulate – how to balance truth and lie in one question. He turned his gaze on the Prince and, pointing to the left-hand door, said: 'If I asked him' (meaning Watt) 'whether that was the right door, would the answer be "Yes"?'

'Yes,' said the Prince. 'Five seconds.'

Swallow worked it out furiously in his head. If he's lying, then Watt's answer truthfully would be 'No'. So it would be the other, the right-hand door. And if he's telling the truth, then Watt, lying, would answer 'Yes' and mean 'No'. So...

'One second.'

'It's the right-hand door,' he said.

'Go and try it,' said the Prince, his face betraying no emotion.

Swallow crossed to the door. He stopped by it for a moment, as if going over the arguments which had forced him to this conclusion. Then he turned the handle and the door swung open.

A narrow shaft of sunlight streamed across the hall, the most beautiful light Swallow had ever seen. And outside the door was a vision of clear blue skies, broad meadows and tall, proud trees – to Swallow a vision of Paradise. He knew without being told that this was England, journey's end, the goal for which he'd been aiming. And now despite difficulties, despite opposition, despite hardship, he had made it. The Prince of Darkness was defeated and must retreat to his traditional boundaries. Night would not cover the earth. His Princess would recover; and perhaps even now she and the rest of the Swallows were setting out from the south to repossess their home. It had taken so long; the issue had for so long been in doubt, that at first Swallow did not quite know what to do or how to react.

No such uncertainty seized the Prince. He cowered away from the glare, the black gold of his crown spraying sparks of sunlight round the hall.

'Seize him and shut that door,' he hissed.

But Swallow stood in the sunlight. None of the Prince's followers was eager to obey the command.

'Watt! Shut the door!' the Prince insisted.

Watt didn't move. Like Swallow, he was framed in the sunlight, his small body casting a long shadow across the hall. And like Swallow he hoped to go through the doorway.

'Shut it!'

Still Watt didn't move. The Prince, black eyes ablaze, seemed to smile at him. The long shadow curled up and crept inside him. The sunlight poured into the hall and now it shone through Watt, casting no shadow. Watt's face crumpled with pain. He let out a howl of agony and staggered across the hall like a wounded animal. The shadow within him moved him against his will to the door. But he fought. He fought heroically. Though racked with pain he planted his feet into the ground as in a tug-of-war and fought every inch of the way. It was all in vain. Bit by bit the shadow edged him nearer to the door. Then he was by it and pushing it to, still resisting – pulling away, only to be jerked back each time to close it a little more, until finally it banged to and the dark of the hall returned to normal.

Watt sagged against the door, spent, defeated. But his master had not done with him. 'Now seize the Swallow and bring him over here.'

Watt levered himself up and moved woodenly over to Swallow's side. He took hold of his wing and started to cross to the Prince.

Swallow pleaded: 'He broke the rules, Watt, you heard him. He made the rules then broke them. He cheated. You mustn't obey him.'

Watt heard what Swallow said and he knew it to be true – every word of it. But he was powerless to act, powerless to speak. When he tried to speak, the shadow scrambled his words. He wanted to say 'I know, but I can't help myself', but all that came out was 'Iouiaaaeieee' – a sound like a tortured cat. He was powerless even to show Swallow that he had heard. He was possessed by the shadow, and he took Swallow across to his master.

'Gag him,' ordered the Prince. 'He's got too much to say for himself.'

Watt reached into his pocket for his handkerchief.

Swallow knew that he had to get through to Watt before he was gagged, or all would be lost: 'I won. You saw me win in a fair contest. He can't stop me now.'

'Oh yes I can. This is *my* kingdom. I can do what I like. What's more, whether he likes it or not, your little friend will help me.'

'Watt! Watt! We're friends! We've been through so much. Don't abandon me now! Watt! It's me, Swallow!'

Watt looked blankly at him. In his pocket his hand grasped the handkerchief, and in doing so brushed against the little bottle. A drop of water from the rim of the bottle transferred itself to his hand. His fingers tingled.

The Prince mocked Swallow: 'You abandoned him, when you threw him off your back. Your friendship is all in the past. The future for him is to be my policeman – in England – under my government.'

Watt's arm, controlled by the shadow, removed the

handkerchief from the pocket and brought it out in front of him, preparatory to folding it into a good gag shape. From inside his head Watt watched, as from a garret window. The tingling spread through his hand. The two hands came together and started folding. His left hand, obedient to the shadow, strove to shape the gag. But his right hand, the tingly one, the one that had touched the water, seemed to be out of control. It would not co-operate in the process. It stayed there, in position, but inoperative – as though awaiting instructions. The tingling spread up his arm.

Watt, not realising what had happened, but aware that something had, decided that it was time to stop being a spectator and to start getting involved. He ordered his hand to drop the gag. It did. He commanded it to clench. As he thought the command, the hand clenched. Watt's face was still blank. But inside his head he smiled. The arm was again under his control.

The Prince and Swallow had fallen silent, spell-bound by this process. Then Swallow, as though awakening from a trance, suddenly cried, 'It's not!'

'What's not?' demanded the Prince, hauling himself back to the business in hand.

'England is not under your government. That's another trick.'

'Gag him. Quick! Stop his talk!' the Prince ordered.

But Watt had other intentions. He now guessed that his arm's liberation must have had something to do with its touching the bottle, and if a drop could do that for his arm, then perhaps... Leaving the captive hand holding the handkerchief uselessly out in front of him, he returned his other hand to his pocket.

Swallow pleaded, trying desperately to reach Watt, but seeing from the expressionless face, no sign that he was succeeding: 'England is in the heart of his dominions, but is not itself under his control. He's lying. Don't you see? Watt? Don't you see?'

Watt's hand found the bottle and took hold of it.

'What happened when I opened the door? Light streamed

in, didn't it? Where from? England! Don't you see what that means? It *can't* be part of his kingdom.'

The Prince tried to intervene. He no longer made any attempt to disguise his fears: this bird's tongue was dangerous. Talk like this could infect the courtiers. 'Silence him!' he cried.

'It's not part of his kingdom. It's not. And you're not his policeman!'

*'Silence him!'*

Watt brought the bottle from his pocket and, before anyone knew what was happening, his arm had carried it to his mouth and he wiped the damp rim across his lips.

The tingling shot through him, starting at his lips and sending shock waves into every corner of his body. Like a rabbit bolting before a fox, the shadow fled. The smile which had been inside his head, spread across his face.

'No,' he said, stunning them all, himself included. He repeated the word to make sure he had heard correctly: 'No. I want to hear.'

Swallow seized his chance: 'England is surrounded by darkness, cut off from the rest of the world, but is not dark itself. It must have held out against him – an island of light. And you are an English policeman. Don't you see? He has no hold over you. He's your enemy as much as he is mine.'

Watt turned to the Prince: 'You said I was your servant. You lied to me.'

'Was or will be – what's the difference?'

'The difference it that I can't obey you. I don't know your law. So I can't enforce it. I thought there was something wrong: if I was your policeman, like you said, I should have been happy obeying your orders. But I never was. Well, now I know why.' He turned and pointed to the door. 'That is the way to England. I am an English policeman. So that's the way I'm going. What's more, my friend is going with me. And if you, or any of your creatures, try to stop us, I shall take you with me and expose you to the light.' He looked severely round the hall for a moment defying them to try; then said, 'Right, Swallow, now. Come on.'

They turned away and started to move to the door. The Prince at once sent his shadows darting after them. But where before those shadows had entered Watt like an empty building, now they found the premises occupied; and not only that, but stoutly defended. Time and again they were repulsed. And Swallow and Watt, secure behind the water's protective glow, moved quickly to their goal.

The Prince fumed with frustration. Uncertainty was replaced by desperation. If he could not beat these pests on his own, then, sooner than let them escape, he would unleash his forces, give them their head and let black anarchy reign. He drew his shadows back into him. For a moment the friends moved freely, thinking they had won. Then, summoning all his power and with a monstrous effort, the Prince shot shadows out all over the hall and the lights, such as they were, went out.

Blackness flooded over Swallow and Watt. And with it came all the forces of the dark. The Wild Wind blew up and tossed them hither and thither. Toads scrabbled at them with spongy fingers. Great Owls swooped down at them with murderous claws. The air was filled with the piping of Bats and the floor covered with Worms. One by one Swallow threw out the remaining orange seeds. But although in the Sahara they had blossomed into great bright branches, here they merely fizzled briefly and died. They were enough, however, to keep the Bats at bay and to enable Swallow and Watt each to see where the other was, and how they were doing. Swallow was faring worst, for their enemies were concentrating on him; Watt was left to the Bats and Worms. But as, ducking to avoid the one, and slipping on the carpet of the other, he spent most of his time on his back, he could offer Swallow no help. Indeed it seemed only a matter of time before he could be covered in the seething bed of Worms and suffocated to death. They squirmed all over him: up his legs, inside his tunic, over his face, up his nose, under his eyelids, in his ears. He struggled and writhed away from them. He thrashed them off. But for every Worm removed another ten squirmed up to take their place. And all his efforts served only to embed him more deeply in the wormy mattress.

Swallow was fast running out of orange seeds. And then what? Would the Worms get him too? Or was he to be blown to the depths of the Maggot midden for them to carve him up at their leisure? Or covered slowly in Bat droppings and allowed to rot from the tail up? That was his fear: to die defenceless, deprived of his right to fight. His blood froze at the thought of what might be in store for him. But he didn't have long to ponder the question, for suddenly something slipped over his head and encircled his chest. Before he could move, it had tightened round him. Then he was swung off his feet and up in the air. He threw out his last orange seed, which shed just enough light for him to see that he was suspended by the Mamba's creeper. The Prince and the Mamba smiled down at him from the balcony. 'Farewell, feathered foe,' hissed the former. And the Mamba, green eyes glowing, almost grinning, looked happy for the first time as he let out the creeper bit by bit.

The light fizzled out and Swallow felt himself descending, bound and helpless. Fat Toad fingers grabbed at him and guided him somewhere. But where? Gummy slobbering mouths sucked at him, covering him with spittle. Bat droppings fell on and around him; and again there came the sinister sound of Maggot knives sharpening. Swallow knew that he was being dressed for dinner. But this time the Maggots made no pretence of waiting till he was dead. Only one thing could save him: the timer, his life-timer. Camel had told him that if he prevailed over the Prince of Darkness and was detained by foul means, then by turning the timer upside down he would be carried to his goal and the dark would be defeated. The conditions were right. He had won. He should now be at home in England. And would have been, had the Prince not cheated. But, stupid bird that he was, now that he wanted the timer, he couldn't reach it. His wings were pinned to his sides and the timer was in his pocket.

The Worms contined to gum him, and the Bat droppings mixed with the spittle to cover him with what was, to a Maggot, a tasty sauce. He had been cheated out of victory.

Now he must cheat in turn.

'Enjoy your dinner,' he cried, 'especially as it will be your last.'

No reply. The lips continued gumming, the droppings dropping. His tail feathers began to dissolve in the juice.

Still no reply. But, perhaps a hopeful sign, no laughter either. No ridicule from Prince and Mamba. Not even, thought Swallow, the silent smile. His feathers fell out of his flesh. Had he left it too late? Then it came – the question he'd been hoping for.

'What do you mean – it will be our last dinner?' the Prince inquired.

'Your old enemy, the Sage of the Sahara, gave me a glass containing the sands of time as a protection. That glass is now in my pocket. And if I die before my time . . .'

'Yes, if you die before your time – what then?'

'What then?' thought Watt, beginning at last to see some significance in the strange hour glass.

'What then, indeed?' thought Swallow, hoping that his powers of invention would not desert him. 'If I die before my time, for every grain of sand that has not fallen through the neck of the glass, one of you will die. I am only a young bird. There are thousands of grains of sand still to drop through. All of you here and many of your followers elsewhere will die. So, though I may not reach England, my Princess will. Darkness will be defeated and the Swallows will, after all, return home. You didn't think I was so foolish as to come here with no protection, did you?'

Watt spat out a mouthful of Worms and prepared to go down fighting. There was more to Swallow than met the eye – much more. They had won. Even if they died, they had won. The world was safe. Survival was no longer the question, but putting up a show. And Watt would put up a show to rank with the greatest of all time – the Spartans at Thermopylae, Horatio defending the bridge, Nelson at Trafalgar, or Wellington at Waterloo.

And up on his balcony the Prince scowled. What was the matter with this bird? Why wouldn't he die quietly?

Whenever he thought he had him defeated, the blessed creature came up with some new confusion. And what was he to make of this latest diversion? It should be a trick; but it could just be true. The bird was innocent enough – he wouldn't have thought of a trick like this on his own. But the Sage of the Sahara – Camel or whatever he now was – had always been a thorn in his side. He wouldn't put anything past him. It was a risk he couldn't take.

'How do I know this isn't a trick?'

(Had Swallow had fingers he would now have crossed them.) 'It says so on the glass.'

'Where is it?'

'In my pocket. You couldn't get them to stop gumming me, could you, just for a minute?'

'Not until I know you're telling the truth. Fetch me the glass!'

Swallow felt fingers fumbling in his pocket.

'Bring it over here. Carefully.'

The glass was removed and Swallow heard one of the Toads cross gingerly to his master.

'Where on the glass? There's nothing here.'

'On the bottom. It says – as far as I can remember – er . . . ?' (Swallow played for time and prayed to Watt's oracular muse for inspiration) '. . . er:

At the end of his day comes the darkness of death . . .

But . . . come darkness at noon, that means death to the dark.'

'Does it indeed? "Death to the Dark", eh? Let's see, shall we?' said the Prince darkly.

And with that, he turned the timer upside down.

# 16

# The Homecoming

As the sands in the glass were overturned and thrown into disorder, so too were the Prince and his followers. It was almost as though they, like the sands, were contained in a glass and the Prince by his action had turned them too upside down and overthrown his own authority.

Pursue that analogy: if you can, picture the Prince's empire, actual and potential, as an hour glass – the Prince, his palace and followers as the sands already settled at the bottom; their victims (Swallow and Watt in this case) as grains trickling through the neck of the glass; and those not yet but soon to be prey to him – for example the rest of the Swallows – the sands funnelling down from the top, slithering helpless to the pit, ready to drop through when their turn came. Then imagine that glass overturned: – the Swallows are no longer potential victims, their world is not at risk; Swallow and Watt stop trickling – they have survived the onslaught; and in the Prince's world, everything is turned upside down and all that he has slips through his fingers and from his grasp.

Even so it was. His empire collapsed. His world came crashing in upon him. Walls of water, stained water windows, heavy doors and high fluted columns became as a thousand waterfalls and cascaded down upon the Prince and his followers. For a moment the air was filled with their screams and howls. Then they were swallowed up in the torrent and swept away.

But though the tempest raged all around them, Swallow and Watt stood firm, caught as it were in the eye of the hurricane. Time swept past them carrying the Prince and his powers back where they belonged. Then the dark, so used to being densely populated with creatures real and imaginary, found itself unaccustomedly empty. Deprived of its usual inhabitants, it could no longer terrify; and not terrifying, it was forced to admit that it was itself scared. It panicked and fled headlong and hopeless into the night. And in its stead came a light which grew and grew until the air was filled with it. The day rejoiced at its deliverance. The Sun beamed down at Swallow and Watt by way of thanking them. Small fluffy clouds jostled them jokingly. And the wind, once more their friend, expressed his gratitude by carrying them, with no help from Swallow, soaring high and free . . . above London.

There was the River Thames curling its way, sparkling by Westminster Abbey and the Houses of Parliament, under London Bridge which was not falling down, and past the Tower still garrisoned by the faithful Ravens. There was Hyde Park, green and lush, there the Old Bailey, topped as ever by golden justice – the silent symbol of Watt's law. And there – Watt's heart skipped a beat – *there* was Piccadilly Circus.

They had done it! How, Watt would never know, but they had. The world was bright again and here they were, home. He hugged Swallow: 'You did it! You did it!'

'*We* did it,' replied Swallow choking, partly from emotion, but more from the fervour of Watt's embrace, '. . . just. Touch and go though, wasn't it?'

'Yes. Touch and go.'

'Sorry about throwing you off. I had to, if we were ever to get here.'

'I wondered about that.'

'Well, I realised, you see, that the Prince of Darkness would only agree to meet opponents who'd had all the stuffing knocked out of them. That way he'd be sure to win, and his followers would think him invincible.'

'Oh . . . is that why he told me that his enemies only saw him when they stopped looking?'

'Of course. We had to convince him that we'd given up

looking, that we were already beaten. Well, I reckoned that if I threw you off, you'd get to meet him at once, since you'd be falling helpless through the void and wouldn't be looking for anyone. Then, if I appeared to be exhausted, which I very nearly was, I'd probably get to meet him too.'

'So it was all thought out?'

'Not all, but most of it.'

'Didn't mean to die, though, did you?'

'No.'

'Lucky we had that magic water . . .'

'But then I didn't die.'

'If it hadn't been for that, you'd still have been dead. I'd have been . . . What did you say?'

'I didn't die.'

'You did. I saw you. You floated down through the water. The Maggots were about to eat you. The magic water brought you back to life.'

'No. I appeared to be dead, but I wasn't – not quite. There's an old folk tale told of Swallows, that we sleep under water. We don't, of course – we sleep in nests, just like other birds. But, if we get terribly cold, our whole system slows down so that we appear to be dead. And in that state we can 'sleep' pretty well anywhere. I thought, if I was going to die anyway, I might as well give it a try. And I just hoped that you would realise what I was up to and find a way to revive me. Which you did, with the magic water.'

'Er . . . no. Not exactly. I . . . the water was an accident. I thought you were . . . But of course. If you weren't dead, that would explain the sand stuck in the neck of the hour glass.'

'Yes.'

'Good old Camel, giving you that. You didn't tell me.'

'He said not to.'

'Just as well. With the hold the Prince had over me, I'd probably have told him everything – all about you dying before your time.'

'No. You'd never have told him that.'

'I might. You saw how I was in his power.'

'Yes, but you still wouldn't have told him that. You see – it wasn't true.'

'What?'

'It wasn't true. I made it up to get him to turn the glass upside down. I had to. Otherwise we'd have been beaten.'

'You mean – if you hadn't got him to turn that glass, we'd have been . . . ?'

Swallow nodded.

'. . . and the world would have gone dark?'

He nodded again: 'That's just what I mean.'

Watt breathed out a long breath: 'I'm rather glad I didn't know.'

'Still friends?' said Swallow.

'Still friends,' said Watt. 'But I can't wait to get down there. Life on the beat should be a piece of cake after this.'

Swallow circled the sky above Eros: 'I suppose this is where we say "Goodbye".'

'Yes. I'd better go. I can feel myself growing already. Go on, drop me off, or I really will drag you down this time.'

'All right,' said Swallow, 'but we're friends. Don't forget.'

'You just try me,' said Watt, now twice the size of Swallow and growing every second. 'Any time you want somewhere to stay, there's always room in my helmet. Same goes for the rest of the Swallows. Go on, turf me off. I'm too big for you now.'

'I'll keep you to that,' said Swallow. 'And when my Princess arrives, we'll come down and see you in Trafalgar Square.'

'Promise?'

'Promise. Goodbye.'

'Goodby-y-y-ye,' called Watt as Swallow rolled over and he dropped away – down – down – down, growing all the time, until he landed feet first and full-size at the foot of Eros.

Swallow waited to see that he was all right, and when Watt looked up to wave farewell, Swallow flew in a big curve over the London roof-tops, down into Leicester Square, along Coventry Street, and past Eros up the splendid, sun-drenched stone of Regent Street. Watt watched him go, then turned to the German tourists who were asking him the way to the Zoo.

'Yes, certainly. Straight up Regent Street, past Oxford Circus, the BBC...'

Up in the sky the Swallows were coming home. And high over Hyde Park Swallow and Princess Hiro were re-united. It was some time before either could think what to say, so they just flew together, wings touching, breath mingling, sharing the moment. Like twin tiny brushes they painted the sky with patterns of love. At last Princess Hiro found her voice: 'I thought you must have died.'

'So I did – once or twice.'

'You were very brave...'

'You wouldn't say that, if you'd seen me trembling in the jungle.'

'... but very silly.'

'Maybe someone had to be.'

'Why you?'

'I was best qualified, I suppose. I mean, if I'd had any brain at all, I'd have known it was impossible and wouldn't have tried it. And then we wouldn't be here now.'

'No.'

'But what I didn't know – what nobody knew – was that I was going to meet Watt.'

'Who?'

'Watt – my friend. I would have died a dozen times without him.'

'I'd like to meet him.'

'I'll introduce you.'

'Good.'

Silence.

'I'm glad you did it.'

'So am I.'

'But promise you won't do it again.'

'I won't be able to. I can't be silly if I'm married to Princess Hiro. It would set a bad example. And anyway, maybe nobody will need to be silly now.'

'Maybe.'

Again their wings touched and the world stopped. For a

moment all life was concentrated in that tiny point of contact. Then the Princess swooped away and soared up with Swallow at her tail.

'Come on,' she said. 'I'll show you the royal apartments.'

'Where are they?' asked Swallow, suddenly feeling small again.

'Windsor Castle. It's wonderful – high up above the River Thames. When the Sun comes up in the morning we're always the first to feel it, and when it goes down at night we're the last to see it go. You'll love it. The Cows and the Crickets will be our orchestra and we'll dance to their music. And then, when the children are growing and we have to stay at home with them – then you can tell us about your adventures.'

'Yes,' said Swallow, 'yes I will. And I'll introduce you to Watt. And when we fly south next winter we'll look in on Hoopoe and Heron in the Vale of Tears, and visit the Tangerines of the Barbary Coast, and we'll holiday with Rhino and play with More and Less and . . . Oh, come on . . .'

And up they flew, up and away into the blue.

'Oh, by the way,' the Princess said as she went, 'when we were flying over the Sahara, I came across a Scorpion who asked to be remembered to you. He sent a message – if I can remember – he said: Not to worry – though a three-legged Camel was at a severe disadvantage, seven legs were more than adequate for a Scorpion. That he had seven good ones and that if you had time, when flying over, he'd always be glad to see you. He said you'd understand. I hope you do. It sounded like gibberish to me.'

'No,' said Swallow, smiling, 'no. Not gibberish. I'll always have time for him.'

Later that year a proud father and mother Swallow paid a visit on a London policeman with their four young children. And ever since, even though the policeman shows no sign of remembering either their adventure or his promise, one or other of them drops in on him and occupies his helmet whenever possible – for old time's sake. And as for the Prince of Darkness – well, he never again tried to take over the world, though he was often sorely tempted. But he still lives in hope. He flexes his muscles every night; and who knows but one day he may again threaten to...

# 17

# When Night Has Fallen

'Uncle Chris! Wake up, uncle Chris!'

'What?'

'Wake up. Come on!'

Sergeant Watt stared uncomprehendingly at the children, who stood impatiently over him. He stared beyond them at the darkening sky, from which all trace of early evening pink had long since vanished.

'Tell! Tell!'

'Tell what?'

'The story of the Swallow and your helmet. You promised.'

He turned his head and stared at the helmet still hanging on its peg on the wall, and at the small head visible over the rim.

'Auntie Sarah says if you come in now, there'll just be time for the story before bed.'

'Does she?'

'Yes. Come on.' They started back up the lawn.

'But I *have* told it. What do you think I've been doing here all this time? Haven't you been listening?'

'Been listening to your snoring,' laughed Tom. 'I think the whole street's been listening to that.'

'Come on,' cried Jenny, 'you can't get out of it. You can't

make rules and then break them. Tell! Tell!' And they raced back indoors.

Sergeant Watt shook himself and took a sip of tea from his mug. It was stone cold. He pulled a face. He eased himself up out of his deckchair. His joints creaking, he started slowly, musingly up the lawn.

'Must have been dreaming . . . funny sort of dream though – so like reality . . . I'd been sitting there explaining – about the Swallows . . .'

But already the dream was slipping away from him.

'. . . there was a Swallow and a policeman . . . what was his name? Watt – that was it . . . funny – my name . . . fair enough in a dream though . . . a trip from Africa to fight the Prince of Darkness. Yes . . . funny sort of dream . . . so real . . . explained about the Swallows too . . . Be good if it were true.'

A line of Shakespeare's came back to him from his schooldays – 'The Tempest' – he'd done it for 'O' level, done it to death, he thought, but this one line had stayed with him:

> 'We are such stuff as dreams are made on . . .'

Was *he* such stuff? Was there truth in the dream? Or had it only *seemed* real?

He went slowly, sore-footedly, stiffly up the lawn. He glanced at the helmet and, as he did so, he could have sworn that the little bird sleeping there opened its eye and winked at him, as much as to say, 'What's real?' He shook himself again and slopped some cold tea down his trousers. Then he went in. No: cold tea was real; stiff joints were real; sore feet and Trafalgar Square – *they* were real.

The rest was imagination.